AF323998

Criminal Justice
Recent Scholarship

Edited by
Nicholas P. Lovrich

A Series from LFB Scholarly

Returning Home
Intimate Partner Violence and Reentry

Matasha L. Harris

LFB Scholarly Publishing LLC
El Paso 2015

Library of Congress Cataloging-in-Publication Data

Library of Congress Cataloging-in-Publication Data

Harris, Matasha L., 1976-
  Returning home : intimate partner violence and reentry / Matasha L.
Harris.
      pages cm. -- (Criminal justice: recent scholarship)
  Includes bibliographical references and index.
  ISBN 978-1-59332-771-2 (hardcover : alk. paper)
  1. African American criminals--Rehabilitation. 2. African American
prisoners--Deinstitutionalization. 3. Intimate partner violence--United
States. 4. Ex-convicts--Family relationships--United States. I. Title.
  HV9304.H324 2015
  364.8089'96073--dc23
                            2014039076

ISBN 978-1-59332-771-2

Manufactured in the United States of America.

Table of Contents

Acknowledgements vii

Introduction 1

Chapter 1: Setting the Stage 11

Chapter 2: The Process 37

Chapter 3: Inside Look From the Outside 47

Chapter 4: More Than a Number: Unveiling the Mask 67

Chapter 5: Violence and Reentry: Their Story 79

Chapter 6: Reflections 117

Appendix A 129

Appendix B 131

References 137

Index 157

Acknowledgements

To the twenty-nine men and women who offered a glimpse into their lives, I am forever grateful. I stand with you. Your voices are not alone.

I am grateful to my editor, Nicholas Lovrich, for his insights and suggestions. To Leo Balk at LFB Scholarly Publishing, thank you.

I thank Gail Garfield for her incredible insight and wisdom during this process. I appreciate you.

To my students at Bowie State University, you inspire me.

Finally, to my mom, family, and my rock, thanks for sharing this incredible journey with me.

Introduction

Mass incarceration of prisoners has inadvertently affected many of the nation's communities; this phenomenon has especially affected the African American community (Mauer, 2011; Hairston & Oliver, 2006). Prisoner populations in the United States are disproportionately black (Glaze & Herberman, 2013), with an overwhelming majority of person incarcerated being young men. As of 2012, an estimated 2.3 million inmates were incarcerated in state and federal prisons and local jails across the United States. Of that number, 1.6 million were serving time in state and federal prisons; African American men and women had the highest rate of imprisonment of any demographic group. African American males had an imprisonment rate that was nearly 6 times that of white non-Hispanic males (Carson & Golinelli, 2013). In some respects, the female inmate population mirrors the male inmate population. African American women were incarcerated at a rate 2.5 times that of white non-Hispanic females (Carson & Sabol, 2012). According to Richie (2012, 2001), the ethnic profile of women in prison represents one of the most vivid examples of racial disparity in our society. By far, the majority of women who are incarcerated in this country are women of color, mainly black and brown women (Carson & Golinelli, 2013).

These statistics place reentry to the community into sharp focus, especially for African American communities. Here prisoner reentry has a disparate impact because many African American communities struggle with persistent poverty, chronic unemployment, high crime rates, and fragile family relations. Hundreds of thousands of African American men and women are returning to their communities from incarceration, in large part without adequate support. In most cases, these are the same economically disadvantaged communities where intimate partner violence (IPV) is more severe and occurs most often (Hairston & Oliver, 2006).

Many prisoners report a history of violence against their intimate partners (White, 2002). Despite this well-documented fact only two published studies (Hairston & Oliver, 2006; Bobbitt, Campbell, & Tate, 2006) have addressed the relationship between prisoner reentry and intimate partner violence. Hairston and Oliver's (2006) study examined the experiences of intimate partner conflict between incarcerated and formerly incarcerated African American men and their wives or girlfriends. A series of focus groups were conducted wherein women participants widely agreed that the experience of imprisonment negatively influences men's behavior as husbands and fathers after their release. For example, exposure to the informal social world of prison culture influenced the incarcerated man's attitude and behavior toward women in such a way that men felt their female partners were obligated to remain unquestionably faithful to them to the extreme. Male participants in the focus groups commonly reported that they were aware of incarcerated men who try to control their intimate partners while inside prison and most consider violence to be an appropriate response to infidelity.

Hairston and Oliver's (2006) study also revealed several sources of conflict that focus group participants believed are likely to lead a man to resort to acts of violence against his intimate partner after he returns home from prison. These sources include rumors of infidelity, economic pressure arising from a sense of lack of household authority, displaced anger about being in prison, the recall of unfulfilled promises, and their partners using supervision of parole as a threat. Male participants also believed violence against women was often justified in order to gain control in the relationship.

Bobbitt, Campbell, and Tate (2006) argue that failure to address intimate partner violence during prisoner reentry can place victims of domestic violence in continued danger and increase formerly incarcerated individual's risk of returning to prison. Their research included roundtable discussions with domestic violence advocates, corrections administrators, staff, and input from African American men and women with first-hand experience of domestic violence and reentry. Several key practices and challenges were identified, including institutional resistance to addressing domestic violence, ways to involve intimate partners, and the value of cultural competence and programming that considers race. Participants also expressed a need for training and ongoing dialogue between criminal justice staff and domestic violence advocates, frequently noting the value of including the perspectives of former victims.

Although intimate partner violence has been identified as an issue for formerly incarcerated individuals during reentry, the majority of attempts to address reentry problems have focused on the other competing challenges that incarcerated men and women commonly encounter. It is well documented that various key resources such as housing, employment, education, and health care are critical factors in post-incarceration success (Taylor-Greene, Polzer, & Lavin-Loucks, 2006; Petersilia, 2004; Richie, 2001; Rose & Clear, 2001; Travis, 2005). Another major challenge that many formerly incarcerated individuals encounter is negotiating social relationships, especially with intimate partners following periods of incarceration. Intimate partner violence can be physical, sexual, emotional, economical, or psychological actions or threats of actions that are detrimental to another person. IPV includes any behavior that intimidates, manipulates, humiliates, isolates, frightens, terrorizes, coerces, threatens, blames, hurts, or physically injures someone (United States Department of Justice, 2012). Little attention, however, has been given to the issue of reentry and IPV by scholars.

For many African American men and women during reentry, IPV frequently becomes a major issue. The majority of men and women released from prison remain under correctional supervision. Engaging in intimate partner violence, especially physical abuse, is a violation of probation conditions and parole supervision. Intimate partner violence during reentry, therefore, has the potential to exacerbate the difficulties and challenges experienced by many African American men and women, further complicating reintegration efforts. Consequently, their inability to adjust and reintegrate successfully into the community can increase their likelihood of recidivating and returning to prison. National recidivism statistics suggests that two-thirds (68%) of released inmates are rearrested within three years, and three-quarters (77%) are rearrested within five years (USDOJ, 2014). Many will return to prison for new crimes or parole violations. Previous literature has examined the correlates of recidivism. These studies document that minority offenders who are young and male are more likely to recidivate than any other demographic group (USDOJ, 2014; Spohn & Holleran, 2002; Benedict et al., 1998; Hepburn & Albonetti, 1994).

This cycle of incarceration and reentry into society carries potential for profound and adverse consequences for African American men and women and the communities to which they return. Yet, there is little scholarship in this area, particularly concerning the specific causes, effects, and implications of intimate partner violence in the lives of black men and women returning to their communities from prison. A deeper understanding of how race, gender, and class shape men's and women's experiences of IPV during reentry is needed in order to provide plausible solutions to improve their reentry outcome, lessen their risk of recidivating, and reduce their chances of becoming a victim. This research addresses this regrettable gap in our knowledge.

Theoretical Framework

The theoretical orientations of restorative justice, critical race theory, and critical race feminism inform this research. These theoretical frames seek to address different dimensions of persistent social inequalities within our society. Collectively, these three theories assist with understanding the ways in which race, gender, and class intersect to structure African American men's and women's experiences of IPV during reentry, and help provide plausible recommendations for addressing this issue. Restorative justice strategies that consider the insights of critical race theory and critical race feminism have the potential to give voice to marginalized groups such as formerly incarcerated African American men and women. The intersection of these three theoretical frames is utilized to help explain the meaning, nature, and challenges of formerly incarcerated African American men's and women's experiences during reentry.

<u>Restorative Justice</u>

Restorative approaches to crime have a long history, dating back thousands of years to the Babylonian Code of Hammurabi (c. 1700 B.C.) which prescribed restitution as a sanction for property offenses. The Sumerian Code of Ur-Nammi (c. 2060 B.C.) also required restitution for offenses of violence (Wilkinson, 1997). Convicted thieves were ordered to pay double the value of stolen goods, as dictated by the Roman Law of the Twelve Tables (449 B.C.). Germanic tribal laws proclaimed by King Clovis (496 A.D.) called for restitution sanctions for both violent and nonviolent offenses, while the Laws of Ethelbert (c. 600 A.D.) included detailed restitution schedules (Wilkinson, 1997). A decisive move away from restorative justice came with the Norman Conquest of much of Europe at the end of the Dark Ages (Van Ness, 1986; Weitekamp, 1998; Wilkinson, 1997). A shift in paradigm occurred whereby crime was no longer perceived as injurious to persons, but rather viewed as an offense against the state, transferring crime into a felony against the King instead of a wrong caused to another person (Braithwaite, 2002). Restitution, a component of restorative justice, is a monetary payment by the offender to the victim for the harm reasonably resulting from the offense (Galaway & Hudson, 1990). In essence, the shift in paradigm signified that restitution was no longer the prescribed sanction. Thereby, restorative justice, restoring the harm that has been caused as a result of a crime, was no longer considered a personal wrongdoing.

The failure of the punitive justice model, excessive use of incarceration, the alienation of victims, and lack of response to their needs generated widespread support for a renewed interest in restorative justice (Braithwaite, 2002; Bazemore, 1999; Clear, 2006). Interest in restorative justice for individual wrongdoing was rekindled in the West by the establishment of an experimental victim-offender reconciliation program in 1974 in Kitchener, Ontario (Peachey, 1989). Restorative justice has been more clearly integrated into criminological thinking as a result of such works as Braithwaite (1989), Zehr (1985, 1995), Umbreit (1985, 1994), and Van Ness (1986). As a consequence of such work, restorative justice became the emerging social movement for criminal justice reform of the 1990s (Daly & Immarigeon, 1998). The restorative justice movement recognized the existence of many situations in which victims and offenders are connected by their life circumstances.

Restorative justice is a philosophy that holds that it is often possible to align the needs of offenders, victims, and the involved community through appropriate forms of interaction and social structures. It is a response to crime that emphasizes healing the wounds of victims, offenders, and communities revealed by criminal behavior

(Hanser, 2010). Core values of restorative justice focus on healing rather than hurting, moral learning, community participation and community caring, respectful dialogue, and the healing power of forgiveness and earned redemption (Nicholl, 1995). Restorative justice involves a way of thinking about crime and its aftermath that asks: Who has been harmed? What are their needs? Whose obligations are these? (Hanser, 2010) Restorative justice shifts the attention toward offenders, victims, and communities with hopes of "restoring" all parties involved.

Restorative justice seeks to restore the offender, victim, and the community to its state of functioning prior to the criminal act, often involving numerous persons in the community in the social reintegration of the offender. By bringing together victims, offenders, families, and key stakeholders in a variety of settings, restorative justice seeks to help offenders understand the implications of their actions and provides an opportunity for them to become reconnected to the community. Thus, restorative justice considers the victims, communities, and the offender as the key participants in the justice process (Hanser, 2010). Three key ideas support restorative justice: (1) victims and community have both been affected and restoration is necessary; (2) offenders' obligation is to make amends with both the victim and the community; and, (3) healing needs to occur for victims as well as offenders (Zehr & Mika, 1998). Both parties are equally important in the healing process to avoid recidivism if possible and restore a sense of safety for the victims.

Restorative justice seeks to provide help for the offender in order to avoid further offenses. In doing so, offenders are encouraged to take responsibility for their actions to repair the harm they have done (Braithwaite, 2002). Restorative justice aims to have a positive impact on offenders by confronting them with the adverse consequences of their actions and clarifying their responsibilities, giving them the opportunity to repair the damage caused to the victim and have them work on finding a solution to their problems (Umbriet, 1994; Fattah, 1998). The most influential text of the restorative justice tradition has been that of Nils Christies' (1977), which defined the problem of criminal justice institutions as "stealing conflicts." The advocates of restorative justice consider crime and wrongdoings to be an offense against an individual and community rather than the State. Alternatively stated, crime is a violation of people and social relationships (Zehr, 1998). As a result, restorative justice involves direct participation of victims and offenders, and prioritizes active involvement of the community. Communities are viewed as direct and indirect victims of crime; therefore, communities are viewed as responsible stakeholders in the ongoing maintenance of social norms.

<u>Critical Race Theory</u>

In developing an understanding of the importance of race in restorative justice, this research draws largely upon the theoretical framework of critical race theory. There are several basic insights associated with critical race theory. One insight instrumental to this study is that "racism is ordinary, not aberrational, normal science, the usual way society does business, the common, everyday experience of most people of color in this country" (Delgado & Stefancic, 2001, p. 7). In other words, structural racial inequalities are not aberrant, but rather the natural order of things. Critical race theory attempts to redress persistent, ongoing social inequalities by studying and transforming the relationship among race, racism, and power (Delgado & Stephanic, 2001) to advance a social justice framework.

Critical race theory draws upon paradigms of intersectionality. Recognizing that race and racism work with and through gender, ethnicity, class, sexuality and/or nation as systems of power, contemporary critical race theory often relies upon and investigates these intersections (Hill-Collins, 2000). Critical race theory examines the many forms of historical and contemporary oppression faced by African Americans. In essence, critical race theory provides a rich foundation for understanding the ways in which race intersects with other forms of social oppression to structure African American men's and women's experiences during the post-incarceration reentry process. The experiential knowledge of African Americans is appropriate, legitimate, and an integral part to analyzing and understanding racial inequality (Delgado & Stefancic, 2001). Critical race theory contends that the perspectives of the oppressed individual or group must be better understood by the larger society. The use of personal narratives contributes to our appreciation of the centrality of African American men's and women's experiences by illuminating their experiences of racial oppression. These stories and the personal narratives associated with them give a voice to a marginalized group which, in many ways has been silenced.

<u>Critical Race Feminism</u>

In developing an understanding of the importance of gender in restorative justice, this research draws largely upon the theoretical framework of critical race feminism (CRF). Critical race feminism helps explain the importance of gender during the reentry process. Much of the current reentry literature overgeneralizes men's experiences, which often reflects the virtual invisibility of women in the field of criminology and criminal justice (O'Brien, 2001; Richie, 2001). Mainstream criminology has been criticized for its lack of attention to women and gender (Britton, 2000; Daly & Chesney-Lind, 1988; Smart, 1976). The reentry experience of women remains largely understudied and poorly documented.

Rooted in critical legal studies, critical race feminism began as a movement with the law and society arena and eventually spread to include other disciplines. As with critical race theory, CRF views racism as ordinary, not aberrational, and uses narratives to construct alternative visions of the reality. Critical race feminism focuses on the oppressed status of women within society (Wing, 1997) and acknowledges that women face systemic inequalities under American institutional structures (Wing, 2003; Allen, 1997; Crenshaw, 1989). Critical race feminism provides insight into the relationship between power and the construction of social roles, as well as the unseen, largely invisible collection of patterns and habits that make up patriarchy and other types of social domination (Delgado & Stefancic, 2001).

Critical race feminism places African American women at the center rather than in the margins or footnotes of analysis (Crenshaw, 1989). While attacking the notion of the essential woman, (based on white middle class women's experience), CRF explores the lives of those facing multiple discrimination on the basis of their race, gender, and class position in society. In doing so, the ways in which race, gender, and class manifest as inequality in society are revealed (Harris, 1990). Critical race feminism seeks to explore and celebrate the differences and diversity among women of color (Matusda, 1992). In reference to violence against women, CRF focuses on the gendered and racialized aspects of such violence, with hopes of developing effective solutions to help women of color.

Integration of Theories

Restorative justice, critical race theory, and critical race feminism are utilized to facilitate a better understanding of the complexities of reentry and IPV for formerly incarcerated African American men and women. Due to the qualitative nature of this work, the intention is not to position men's and women's experiences within a particular theory, but rather to utilize the aforementioned theories as a backdrop for understanding their experiences. Collectively, these theories give meaning to and contextualize men's and women's experiences of IPV during reentry.

Outline of the Book

This book is divided into five chapters and features an appendix section. *Chapter One: Setting the Stage,* begins with a comprehensive overview of the issues of reentry and IPV. Next a discussion of prisoner reentry and the challenges formerly incarcerated men and women encounter is discussed. Afterwards, a discussion of intimate partner violence is given. A discussion of the three main restorative justice initiatives follows. Finally, an examination of why restorative justice is essential and must be considered when attempting to understand the complexities of reentry and IPV for African American men and women is provided.

Chapter Two: The Process, begins with a discussion of the methodological framework, which includes the core dimensions of intersectionality and comparative analysis. The field research methods and data collection processes employed are then discussed in considerable detail. The chapter concludes with a discussion of grounded theory as a means of structuring the data analysis carried out in this study.

Chapter Three: Inside Look From the Outside, begins with an overview of the staff members included in the research. Next, a discussion of the major challenges and issues of reentry as identified by staff members is provided. Also included is a discussion of staff members' perspectives on how race, gender, and class all combine to shape African American men's and women's frequent experiences of intimate partner violence during reentry. The chapter concludes with a discussion of organizational barriers in addressing the needs of the formerly incarcerated men and women affected by the mass incarceration phenomenon.

Chapter Four: More Than a Number: Unveiling the Mask, begins with an analysis of the intake data that provides a general profile of the men and women who sought services through the Fortune Society from January 2008 to September 2011. Afterwards, a profile of participants' demographics, educational attainment, employment, criminal history, and housing arrangements are discussed. A brief biographical sketch of each participant is also given.

Chapter Five: Violence and Reentry: Their Story, begins with an overview of the organization of data. Secondly, the major challenges and issues encountered by African American men and women during reentry are discussed. In doing so, themes that emerged from each of the cases are described in considerable detail. Themes are presented and accompanied by rich quotes representing participants' experiences and perspectives. Lastly, a comparative analysis of the men's and women's experiences is given.

Reflections, the last chapter, provides a summary overview of the study, the principal findings, theoretical implications, and contribution to the literature. A number of suggestions for future research in this area are set forth as a stimulant to additional study and scholarship in this important area of Criminal Justice research.

CHAPTER 1

Setting the Stage

INTRODUCTION

Several scholars have highlighted the challenges of formerly incarcerated African Americans during reentry (Taylor-Greene et al., 2006; Petersilia, 2004; Richie, 2001; Rose & Clear, 2001; Travis, 2005). A major challenge that many encounter is negotiating social relationships, especially with intimate partners following periods of incarceration. Oftentimes during the reentry process the problem of intimate partner violence (IPV) becomes an issue for men and women who seek to restore their lives. Despite the commonplace nature of this problem, there is little scholarship in this area, particularly concerning the specific causes, effects, and implications of intimate partner violence in the lives of black men and women returning to their communities from prison.

Specifically, this research compares African American men's and women's experiences of intimate partner violence during the reentry process. This study explores the ways in which race, gender, and class intersect to structure their experiences during reentry. By comparing the experiences of African American men and women during reentry, this study provides an understanding of gender differences and the role that intimate partner violence plays in shaping those differences.

PRISONER REENTRY AND IPV

Many prisoners report a history of violence against their intimate partners (White, 2002), however only two studies (Hairston & Oliver, 2006; Bobbitt, Campbell, & Tate, 2006) have addressed the relationship between prisoner reentry and intimate partner violence. Although both of these important studies focused on issues of intimate partner violence, neither study included formerly incarcerated women. Hairston and Oliver (2006) examined the experiences of intimate partner conflict between incarcerated and formerly incarcerated African American men and their wives and girlfriends. A series of focus groups were conducted and women participants agreed that the experience of imprisonment negatively influences men's behavior as husbands and fathers after release. For example, exposure to the informal social world of prison culture adversely affected the incarcerated man's attitude and behavior toward women, whereby men believed their female partners were obligated to remain unquestionably faithful to them. Additionally, male participants reported that they were aware of incarcerated men who sought to control their intimate partners while inside prison or who consider use of violence to be an entirely appropriate response to infidelity. For example, many focus group participants acknowledged that it was not uncommon for accusations of unfaithfulness to escalate to various forms of harassment or even threats of and use of violence.

The study revealed several sources of conflict that focus group participants believed are likely to lead a man to resort to acts of violence against his intimate partner after he returns home from prison. These sources include rumors of infidelity, economic hardship, lack of household authority, displaced anger about having been in prison, remembering unfulfilled promises, and their partner's use of revocation of parole as a threat. Similarly, Fishman (1990) observed that incarcerated men often experience significant levels of conflict with their intimate partner, both during and following their incarceration. She noted that the separation caused by imprisonment can heighten the stress that often contributes to intimate partner violence and this type of violence is often times a way to vent frustration.

Although Hairston and Oliver's (2006) study is one of the few studies to examine reentry and domestic violence, there are several issues worth noting. First, as with many reentry studies, the sample did not include formerly incarcerated or incarcerated women. Secondly, the use of focus groups for such a personal topic as intimate partner violence could have been examined in greater depth with the use of qualitative interviews. Lastly, their study was not attentive to the interactions of race, gender, or class in the experiences of their participants.

Bobbitt, Campbell, and Tate (2006) argued that failure to address intimate partner violence during prisoner reentry can place victims of domestic violence in continued danger and increase the formerly incarcerated individual's risk of returning to prison. Their field research included roundtable discussions with domestic violence advocates, corrections administrators, staff, and input from African American men and women with first-hand experience of domestic violence and reentry to address intimate partner violence when men return from prison. Several key practices and challenges were identified, including institutional resistance to addressing domestic violence, ways to involve intimate partners, and the value of cultural competence and programming that considers race. Participants also expressed a need for training and ongoing dialogue between criminal justice staff and domestic violence advocates, noting the particular value of including the perspectives of former victims.

The findings from Bobbitt, Campbell, and Tate's (2006) study provide greater insight into the challenges associated with addressing domestic violence. Although this study included key stakeholders and input from African American men and women who have experience with domestic violence during reentry, the men and women represented the same individuals that were involved in Hairston and Oliver's study (2006). As a consequence, similar issues existed with their methodological design.

Relatively few studies exist that address the complexities of intimate partner violence during reentry. Although Hairston and Oliver (2006) and Bobbitt, Campbell, and Tate (2006) studies acknowledged that IPV is a problem that needs to be addressed, further research is needed to understand how formerly incarcerated African American men and women experience IPV during reentry. Furthermore, a deeper understanding of how race, gender, and class collectively shape men's and women's experiences of IPV during reentry is needed in order to provide plausible recommendations to improve their reentry outcome, diminish their risk of recidivating, and reduce their chances of becoming a victim of intimate partner violence.

PRISONER REENTRY

In 2011, 688,384 men and women- approximately 1,885 individuals a day- were released from state or federal custody (Carson & Sabol, 2012). Prisoner reentry, the process of managing the transition from imprisonment to community reintegration, has been researched quite extensively. There is a wealth of research that argues the formerly incarcerated individual's need for social supports, such as housing, employment, healthcare, and medical treatment and often only poorly addressed (Taylor-Greene et al., 2006; Urban Institute, 2006; Marbley & Ferguson, 2005; Petersilia, 2004; Metraux & Culhane, 2004; Rose & Clear, 2001). Generally, men and women enter U.S. prisons with limited marketable work experience, low levels of educational, a narrow range of skills, and serious health-related problems ranging from mental health issues to substance abuse histories (Urban Institute, 2006). When they leave prison, these challenges often remains as serious problems. The impact of incarceration is further compounded by their criminal conviction. The unintended consequences associated with a criminal conviction have a direct impact on critical areas of life such as, employment, housing, public benefits, and parental rights that might reduce the ability to reintegrate successfully (Rose & Clear, 2001).

More specifically, women with criminal records who face competing demands are arguably in one of the worst positions to secure services they need due to their community-based resources being seriously limited and their criminal record further inhibiting their access to education, training, and services (Richie 2012, 2001). Formerly incarcerated African American women tend to reside in economically distressed and disorganized neighborhoods with limited social, economic, and political resources. They lack access to programs and services needed to address their underlying problems. As a result, African American women are often marginalized within the context of an economically distressed community because of structural racism, economic exploitation, and political disenfranchisement which makes successful reintegration within the community difficult (Richie, 2012).

Finding and maintaining employment, securing housing, obtaining healthcare services, and rebuilding social networks are significant barriers to formerly incarcerated African American men and women during the reentry process. In order to fully understand the myriad of issues and challenges they encounter when returning to their communities, it is important to understand and recognize underlying socioeconomic factors that influence their life chances prior to entering the prison system. Blacks in the United States have struggled perennially for equality, in terms of employment, housing, healthcare, and education. Seemingly this struggle tends to be a result of historical and institutionalized racial and class discrimination (Potter, 2008). Michelle Alexander (2010) argues that these increasingly severe penalties impacting African Americans represents a modern day version of Jim Crow, legalizing discrimination against swaths of African Americans in employment, housing, access to education, and public benefits at a time when racial prejudice is formally outlawed. Class strongly influences individual access to employment, housing, healthcare, and higher education. Specifically, the areas of greatest need for formerly incarcerated tend to include the following: employment, housing, substance abuse treatment, healthcare, and the rebuilding of supportive social networks.

Employment

Disproportionately, African Americans experience high rates of socioeconomic disadvantage. Poverty among African Americans is persistently high. According to the U. S. Census Bureau's 2011 Annual Social and Economic Supplement, of the 46.2 million people living in poverty, the poverty rate for African Americans was higher than any other ethnic group. Over a quarter of African Americans (27.4%) are poor; one- in-four African Americans lives in poverty. This is not surprising since unemployment is significantly connected to the likelihood of living in poverty. The Bureau of Labor Statistics indicates the African American unemployment rate is traditionally higher than that of any other group. This remains true today; in April 2012, the unemployment rate for African Americans was 13% while the unemployment rate for whites was 7.4 percent (Bureau of Labor Statistics, 2012).

There is also a gender gap between African American men and women in the workforce. The unemployment rate for African American men in April 2012 was 13.7% compared to 10.1% for African

American women (Bureau of Labor Statistics, 2012). African American men and women face severe limitations in access to the opportunity structure –namely, gainful employment. Finding and maintaining a job is a critical dimension for success for formerly incarcerated men and women during the reentry process (Travis, Solomon, & Waul, 2001).

Research has shown that employment is associated with lower rates of re-offending, with higher wages being associated with lower rates of criminal activity (Bernstein & Houston, 2000). Finding a decent paying job can allow formerly incarcerated offenders to succeed in overcoming environmental challenges, in the communities to which they tend to return, problems such as poor education, job training, and skills in largely disenfranchised communities (Marbley & Ferguson, 2005). Formerly incarcerated individuals tend to face tremendous challenges in finding and maintaining legitimate job opportunities because of their low levels of education, limited work experience, and limited range of vocational skills (Harlow, 2003). Their criminal record can be a major obstacle to employment opportunities in many areas of potential employment. Employers are reluctant to hire formerly incarcerated individuals because of their criminal background, and this serves as another barrier to job placement (Holzer, Raphael, & Stoll, 2004).

The types of jobs available to formerly incarcerated individuals are normally low paying and highly unstable. Often they work few hours and therefore do not qualify for benefits such as health insurance. As a result, many may work more than one job or remain unemployed and rely on family for support (Rose & Clear, 2001). In essence, formerly incarcerated men and women alike often return to communities with limited financial resources, but with many financial needs (Rose & Clear, 2001) for which finding a job with a livable wage is difficult. African Americans with criminal records are doubly branded, the penalty of their delinquent status amplified by their racial identity (Martin, 2013).

Finding any job poses unique challenges for both men and women. Male participants in Hairston and Oliver's (2006) study acknowledged that finding employment and a place to live is crucial; meeting these needs is the necessary foundation for coping with the other competing challenges associated with reentry. For men, the lack of a decent job can complicate efforts to reunite with a wife or a girlfriend, particularly if they are expected to be the provider. Pager (2007) found that African

American men with a felony record were "called back" for job interviews less than 5% of the time- this was in contrast to white males with a felony who were three times (17%) more likely to be called back.

Housing

One of the most immediate challenges facing prisoners upon their release is to secure housing. According to the National Governors Association for Best Practices report (2004) on the challenges and impact of prisoner reentry, at least 10% of returning prisoners are homeless both before and after their incarceration. Many have plans to stay with family, as Baer et al. (2006) has shown. The majority of returning prisoners live with family members and/or intimate partners upon their release. Previous research has found that formerly incarcerated individuals who lack stable housing are more likely to return to prison (Metraux & Culhane, 2004) as it represents an outcome that is typically preceded by inadequate resources. Homeless people may resort to illegal activities as a means of survival (Snow, Baker, & Anderson, 1989).

Housing is an especially important issue for unmarried women with children; it is nearly impossible for some to reunite with their children unless they have safe and stable housing. Laws prohibiting persons with felony drug convictions from living in public housing, for example, make reunification extremely difficult for many offenders (Petersilia, 2003; Rubenstein & Mukamal, 2002). Moreover, entire families may be evicted by housing authorities for the drug involvement of a single member, so families in public housing who allow a woman recently released from prison to reside with them may put the tenancy of the entire family in jeopardy (Robbins, Martin, & Surratt, 2009). Securing housing is an issue for men and women offenders alike. Without stable housing, men and women will have a difficult time "restoring" other aspects of their lives.

Substance Abuse

Eighty percent of the prison population has a history of substance abuse (NGA, 2004). Correctional treatment availability for drug and alcohol problems falls short of the documented need for treatment in general (Lurigio, 2000), and there are far fewer treatment programs provided in women's correctional facilities than in men's (Anderson, 2003; Baugh, Bull, & Cohen, 1998; Belknap, 2000; Chesney-Lind, 1997). Although some institutions may offer substance abuse programs, only a small percentage of women who need them have access to such programs (Richie, 2001). Furthermore, programs offered to women tend to be transplants of programs developed for male offenders, with little or no consideration of the special needs and circumstances of women, especially mothers (Robbins, Martin, & Surratt, 2009). In their study of incarcerated women Richie and Johnson (1996) found that for women who completed drug treatment the short-term intervention provided in prison did not adequately prepare them to abstain from substance abuse or manage addiction once released. Few offenders continue to receive appropriate treatment once they reenter the community (Gaes, Flanagan, Motluk, & Stewart, 1999) due to lack of available programming and termination of Medicaid while incarcerated. Therefore, it is not surprising that substance abuse among formerly incarcerated individuals presents significant challenges to the reentry process.

Health

The prevalence of severe mental health as well as chronic and infectious disease among the prison population is far greater than among the general population (Clear, Cole, Reisig, Petrosino, 2015). Since the deinstitutionalization movement of the 1960's, which emphasized the depopulation of large-scale mental hospitals, jails and prisons began to see increasing numbers of the mentally ill within their confines. Over 50% of all inmates have a history of mental problems. (Clear, Cole, Reisig, Petrosino, 2015). According to the National Governors Association Center for Best Practices report (2004), prisoners are between two to four times more likely to be schizophrenic, depressed, bipolar, or suffering from post-traumatic stress disorder than the general population. At midyear 2005, nearly three-quarters (73%) of women in state prison had mental health problems, compared to 55% of men (James & Glaze, 2006); 78% of women incarcerated have a history of physical or sexual abuse (USDOJ, 2001) compared to 10% of men (USDOJ, 1999).

Health data indicate that race is one of the most significant predictors of health and well being. African Americans have high rates of many diseases and one of the fastest growing health risks to African Americans is HIV/AIDS. African Americans, however, are more likely to have inadequate health insurance coverage, and more likely to use hospital emergency rooms as their usual source for medical care (The Henry Kaiser Foundation, 2007).

By the end of 2010, over 20,000 state and federal inmates had HIV or AIDS. The rate of state and federal inmates with AIDS is more than twice as high as the rate in the U.S. population (Clear, Cole, Reisig, Petrosino, 2015). Increased levels of high-risk behaviors help to explain this rate. AIDS is the second leading cause of death in state prisons. While in prison, inmates receive physical and mental health services; however, after release their access to community-based health care tends to be extremely limited (Hammet, Roberts, & Kennedy, 2001). Additionally, incarceration disqualifies inmates from Medicaid eligibility and the process of restoring eligibility can take several months, interrupting access to prescription drugs and putting individuals at high risk of relapse during that process.

Families

Rebuilding social networks is another challenge formerly incarcerated individuals commonly encounter. Social networks are important and play an essential role in their successful transition from prison back into the community. Strengthening the family network and maintaining supportive family contact can improve outcomes for both family members and prisoners alike (Sullivan, Mino, Nelson, & Pope, 2002). Likewise, most prisoners believe that family support is an important factor that can help them stay out of prison. Without social networks in place, formerly incarcerated individuals have little social support upon which to rely. In some cases, the separation caused by incarceration has interfered and disrupted vital networks; many marriages end during incarceration (Hairston & Oliver, 2006).

In addition to the disruption caused by incarceration, social networks suffer another serious strain: formerly incarcerated men have to relearn how to be husbands and fathers (Rose & Clear, 2001). Moreover, many fathers are released from prison and owe substantial amounts of child support (NGA, 2004). Hairston and Oliver (2006) found that relationships with children and their mothers represent another common source of conflict for incarcerated men. Some of the conflict is attributed to the incarcerated father's fear of the girlfriend or spouse allowing another man to become a father figure for his children. In Hairston and Oliver's (2006) study, men reported that conflict with an estranged wife or girlfriend can negatively affect ones relationship with any children the couple may have in common.

Unique challenges exist for women adjudicated offenders as well. Nearly 80% of women in prison have children, compared to 60% of the men in prison. Between 60-70% of these women have one or more children under the age of eighteen (Frost, Greene, & Pranis, 2006); however, women are often incarcerated too far from families for frequent visits, especially for their children (Rose & Clear, 2001). Most significantly, women offenders are likely to have been custodial parents just before their incarceration, and they anticipate resuming the care of their children upon release from prison. This anticipation is not always realized (Bloom, 1993; Harm & Phillips, 2001; Mumola, 2000; Pelisser & Jones, 2005). Consequently, reunification with children is oftentimes another major challenge for incarcerated mothers returning home.

Upon release, the process of reunification between the mother and child is a difficult task. The legal parameters that govern the relationship make it exceptionally hard for the mother and her children who are anticipating the reunification. In many cases, by the time the mother is released her parental rights may have been terminated (WPA, 2003). Forty eight states allow parental rights to be terminated for felony offenders, and eighteen states may terminate a parent's rights for long term prison confinement "which deprives the child of a normal home life or produces negative effects on the parent-child relationships" (Buckler & Travis 2003, p. 442). Approximately ten percent have children in foster care or in other institutions (Harrison & Beck, 2006). If the child or children are not already in the care of the state, many women stand to lose their children shortly after being released due to the challenges of reentry, such as obtaining gainful employment, securing suitable housing, or completing court-ordered treatment programs (WPA, 2003). Restoring these relationships, reunifying with family, and taking on these roles and assuming those responsibilities upon return pose a substantial set of challenges for women offenders in reentry (Travis, Cincotta, & Solomon, 2003).

In summary, there is a wealth of research that argues that formerly incarcerated individuals need social supports including housing, employment, obtaining healthcare, and medical treatment. The majority of studies have focused on men's experiences during reentry with the exception of studies such as those of Richie (2001) and WPA (2003; 2008) who have focused specifically on women's experiences. A few studies have examined the role of race in shaping experiences, such as Hairston and Oliver's (2006) study of black men's experiences of domestic violence and Pager's (2007) study examining challenges during reentry across racial categories. Although a few studies have examined racial and gender differences, what is still unknown is how race, gender, and class intersect to shape formerly incarcerated African American men's and African American women's life chances, opportunities and experiences- particularly, their experiences relating to intimate partner violence during reentry.

INTIMATE PARTNER VIOLENCE

Domestic violence is a pattern of coercive behavior often including physical violence, often involving economical, emotional, sexual, and psychological abuse with or without a physical violence element. Comment elements are isolation, threats, and intimidation perpetrated against their intimate partner and loved ones. Intimate partner violence (IPV), a form of domestic violence, is violence committed by a spouse, ex-spouse, or current or former boyfriend or girlfriend (Centers for Disease Control, 2012). Intimate partner violence can be physical, sexual, emotional, economic, or psychological actions or threats of actions that jeopardize another's personhood. IPV includes any behavior that intimidates, manipulates, humiliates, isolates, frightens, terrorizes, coerces, threatens, blames, or physically injures someone (United States Department of Justice, 2012).

Intimate partner violence is a serious problem in America and occurs among heterosexual and same-sex couples alike. Both men and women are victims of intimate partner violence; however, the majority of all intimate partner violence in the U.S. is perpetrated by men against women. According to estimates from the National Crime Victimization Survey, of approximately 700, 000 victimizations by intimate partners in 2006 about 73% were against women and the remaining 27% involved violence against men (Bureau of Justice Statistics, 2006). Based on the National Violence Against Women Survey, an estimated 5.3 million IPV victimizations occur among U.S. women ages 18 and older each year. This violence results in nearly two million injuries, more than 550,000 of which require medical attention (CDC, 2003). Studies show that women are at greater risk of being harmed by an intimate partner than by a stranger (Centers for Disease Control, 2012; Tjaden & Thoennes, 1998).

Although there appears to be a general understanding that IPV is a serious problem, few seem to agree on the magnitude of the problem (Centers for Disease Control, 2012). Tjaden & Thoennes (2000) argue that the magnitude of IPV is underestimated due to unreported incidents of IPV. Thus, it is believed that available data greatly underestimate the true magnitude of the problem; however, it is also argued that the magnitude of the problem is exaggerated. This is in part due to the lack of consensus about terminology, methodology, gaps in data collection, victims' reluctance to report victimization, the repetitive nature of IPV, and survey limitations (CDC, 2003). Researchers continue to be limited by insufficient data concerning the incidence and prevalence of intimate partner violence. The lack of consistent information about the incidence and prevalence of intimate partner violence limits our ability to understand and respond to the problem. Despite the disagreement and lack of consistent information, what we do know about its frequency of occurrence from the domestic violence literature is sufficient for concern.

Race Matters

Intimate partner violence occurs regardless of education, income level, or geography and is an issue that effects many racial, ethnic, and cultural groups (Cazenave & Straus, 1990; Campbell & Soeken, 1999); that said, yet there are dramatic statistics related to African Americans that cannot be ignored (Bent-Goodley, 2005). In comparison with other racial, ethnic, and cultural groups, African Americans are more likely to be killed or to sustain serious injury because of intimate partner violence (Fagan, 1996; Rennison & Welchans, 2002). Although somewhat controversial, empirical evidence suggests that the most severe and lethal domestic violence occurs disproportionately among low-income women of color, and particularly African American women (Benson & Fox, 2004; Raphael, 2000; Rennison & Planty, 2003). Conversely, several studies (Hampton et al., 1998; Rennison & Planty, 2005) have found that when socioeconomic factors are controlled, racial and ethnic differences in the rate of intimate partner violence largely disappear. As Sokoloff and Dupont (2005) assert, this finding suggests that one of the underlying reasons for the greater level of intimate partner violence among African Americans is not attributable to racial and cultural factors, but rather to high levels of poverty in African American communities. Women who experience the highest rates of non-lethal partner violence are African American women between the ages of 16-24, who live in rental housing, and in urban areas (Campbell, 2003). This demographic profile parallels that of African American males with the highest rates of incarceration (Rose & Clear, 2003).

Intimate partner violence has been found to be more prevalent among African American families (Tjaden & Thoennes, 2000), and the threat of intimate partner violence is particularly dire within the African American community (Hairston & Oliver, 2006). "African Americans are more likely than members of other racial groups to be involved in domestic homicides characterized by a reciprocal pattern of abuse (Hairston & Oliver, 2006)." Nevertheless, African Americans resist requesting support from formal systems of care, such as the criminal justice and social service systems (Bent-Goodley, 2001, 2003; Joseph, 1997; West, 1999; Garfield, 2005). Because of racial loyalty, "African American women may withstand abuse and make a conscious self-sacrifice for what she perceives as the greater good of the community, but to her own physical, psychological, and spiritual detriment" (Bent-Goodley, 2001, p. 323). The silence of abuse is substantiated on the basis of the need to protect African American men from further discriminatory treatment and to not feed into negative stereotypes about African Americans (Bent-Goodley, 2003). As Garfield (2005) acknowledges, African American women's attitudes about and perceptions of interpersonal violence may differ from mainstream definitions. Garfield found that physical aggression was not always viewed as violence by African American women. Nevertheless, African Americans are more likely to be arrested, prosecuted, and incarcerated because of domestic violence events (Richie, 1996; Roberts, 1994).

RESTORATIVE JUSTICE INITIATIVES

For the last 30 years, the advocates of restorative justice have represented a relatively quiet voice in the background of U.S. society. It is only within the last decade or so that the ideas of restorative justice have begun to resonate with noteworthy impact among the general public (Clear, 2006). Today, the concept of restorative justice draws considerable attention from a diverse set of societal stakeholders. There are many examples of successful restorative-justice inspired programs. Based on the principles and elements of restorative justice, several impressive initiatives have been developed which are aligned with the restorative justice philosophy. Restorative justice initiatives engage those who are harmed, wrongdoers, and their affected communities in search of solutions that promote repairing, reconciliation, and the rebuilding of trusting relationships (Van Ness & Strong, 2015; Braithwaite, 2002). Restorative justice seeks to build partnerships to reestablish mutual responsibility for creating and sustaining constructive responses to wrongdoing within communities. Restorative justice seeks a balanced approach to the needs of the victim, the offender, and the community through processes that preserve the safety and promote dignity of all.

Restorative justice programs may be initiated at any point in the criminal justice system, by police, courts, corrections, or during parole. A variety of interactive strategies have been employed; however, for the sake of creating an overview on the successful application of the philosophy models of restorative justice can be grouped into three primary categories: *victim-offender mediation, conferencing, and circles* (Van Ness & Strong, 2015; Bazemore & Umbriet, 1995, Zehr & Mika, 1998; Fattah, 1998). All of these model strategies give victims of crime a more prominent role in the process of deciding what penalty should be constructed in order to meet the aims of restorative justice (Clear, 2006).

Victim-Offender Mediation

In victim-offender mediation programs and schemes, the offender meets with the victim to discuss the offense and determine the ways in which the harm can be repaired. The victim has the opportunity to ask questions of the offender and to describe how they have been affected by the incident. The mediation can also include family members of the offender and the victim (Van Ness & Strong, 2015; Bazemore, 2005; Bazemore & Umbreit, 2001; Umbriet, 1994).

Sentencing Circles

In sentencing circles, the offender must be held accountable, the offender must give back in the way prescribed by the victim to make amends, and the offender must give back to the community. The community is accountable to the victim by assisting and enforcing any specific reparations agreed upon by the victim and the offender by helping the person avoid committing any more crime. Sentencing circles are community-based practices whereby the circle agrees on an acceptable restoration. The offenders have to restore the cost, or provide some kind of appropriate compensation. The circle has regular meetings to discuss progress toward earned redemption, any troublesome issues, and ultimately attempt to restore justice to all parties (Van Ness & Strong, 2015; Stuart, 1996).

Family group conferencing

Family group conferencing involves a wider circle of participants than victim-offender mediation, adding people connected to the primary parties such as family, friends, and pertinent social services professionals. Family group conferences are aimed primarily at young offenders and help engage family and friends of the victim and the offender in a dialogue in order to find the best ways of dealing with past criminal behavior (Van Ness & Strong, 2015; Maxwell & Morris, 1993; Umbreit & Zehr, 1996).

Limitations/Criticisms

Despite the progress that has been made, restorative justice is not exempt from criticism. Often critical, yet constructive, research has been offered by scholars such as Walgrave (2003), Daly (2003), and, Sherman (2000). Evaluations of restorative justice programs are somewhat mixed in their determination of outcomes. Programs such as victim-offender mediation generally increase both victim and offender satisfaction with the process over what would normally be a court-based adverserial process (Latimer, Dowden, & Muise, 2001; Umbriet, Bradshaw, & Coates, 1999). While research shows that victims generally benefit from restorative justice, it must be acknowledged that evaluative research has focused primarily on meditation programs (Walgrave, 1993; Fattah, 1998; Miers, 2001).

Critics of restorative justice sometime contend that victims are not the central focus in the very programs designed to give them a bigger role (Marshall & Merry, 1990; Dignan, 2003). Whether the chosen method is mediation, family conferences, or some other practice, critics note that too many victims are relegated to the role of facilitator or are used as a pretext for pursuing an educational initiative for offenders (Roberts & Roach, 2003; Daly, 2003). Victims are sometimes not involved because they were not invited or could not be reached (Dignan, 2003). Critics point out that restorative programming is limited, due to the voluntary participation from victims, offenders, and the community. In particular, in many offenses the victim may have no interest. Others argue that restorative practices might divert resources away from rehabilitation programs that have a better track record of success in reducing recidivism.

Using restorative justice programs in cases of violent crime is also an issue for some critics. The public and victims generally support the restorative justice model (Bazemore, 1999), but tend to be very reluctant to accept restorative justice in cases of serious violent crimes (Reeves, 1989; Roberts, 2002). Feminists and women's anti-violence advocates have been critical of the use of restorative justice in the domestic violence area (Cameron, 2006). Feminist critiques of restorative justice focus mainly on intimate partner violence and have raised valid concerns with restorative justice in these particular cases. Zehr (2003) argues that domestic violence is probably the most problematic area of application. Likewise, Acorn (2004) argues that in emphasizing forgiveness and the achievement of reconciliation, restorative justice would be inappropriate in cases of sexual violence and is contradictory to vindicating a victim's suffering. In situations where the offender is repeatedly violent or the relationship with the victim is characterized by domination, tyranny or manipulation, criminal victimization means a loss of power or affirmation of a lack of power (Hudson, 2003). For those reasons, feminists, women's anti violence advocates, and victim support groups generally resist and frequently criticize the use of restorative justice programs.

Critics typically emphasize power imbalances, victim safety, and the potential for re-victimization in an informal process (Stubbs, 2007; Daly & Stubbs, 2006; Coker, 2002, Strang & Braithwaite, 2002). In cases of violence against women, their stance evokes strong opposition considering the risk of guarding that type of crime behind closed doors, thereby increasing existing power imbalances. Feminists argue that gendered power imbalances between the survivor and the abuser, cultural and economic factors that exacerbate the subordination of women, and administrative shortcomings that jeopardize the safety of survivors of violence make the use of restorative justice problematic in the IPV realm (Cameron, 2006).

In sum, restorative justice is a social movement that has become very influential. Numerous restorative justice practices are implemented in countries such as Australia, Canada, New Zealand, and the United States. Despite increased attention given to restorative justice, considerable debate has surfaced regarding the applicability of restorative justice to cases involving intimate partner violence. Feminists and women's anti-violence advocates are concerned that as an informal process, restorative justice may re-privatize male intimate violence after decades of feminist activism to make it a public issue which law enforcement and the courts must address head-on.

RESTORATIVE JUSTICE AND REENTRY

Restorative justice is a philosophy that acknowledges that the offender needs to be "restored" when returning to the community. As such, prisoner reentry, the process of managing the transition from incarceration to the community, recognizes that there are challenges that formerly incarcerated individuals encounter. In order to start rebuilding, certain aspects of their lives have to be rekindled, primary among them are intimate partner relationships. The goals of reentry are aligned with the basic elements and philosophical underpinnings of restorative justice. Reentry seeks to maximize offender readiness for release from prison, maintain individual success in the community once the offender is released from prison, and protect and support the community to which the individual returns. One of the goals of reentry and restorative justice is to prevent re-offending and deter other potential crimes (Van Ness & Strong, 2015; Braithwaite, 1999).

Implicit in the restorative justice philosophy is the idea that one important purpose of the criminal sanction is reintegrating the offender into the community following their acceptance of personal responsibility for the harm done to the victim and community (Travis, 2000). A restorative justice approach represents significant new processes for defining the terms of reentry, where the negotiation of relationships among the parties affected by the crime results in a new contract. The victim, the family, and the offender have a direct role in negotiating the contract and consequently an interest in its enforcement (Travis, 2000). An important characteristic of restorative justice is the idea of discussion, dialogue, and negotiation between the parties involved and affected by a given crime (Daly, 1999).

Complexities of Reentry & IPV: Intersectionality

Since the days of slavery in the United States race has been a determining factor regarding opportunities for people of African descent. Race is central to understanding the experiences of black men and women. Historically, African Americans have been discriminated against based primarily on the color of their skin. Race has a complex impact on sense of self, experiences, and life chances of black men and women. Their lives are greatly shaped by race, and in order to examine their reentry experiences it is critical to understand the meaning and the significance of race. Race structures the opportunities, resources, and power for some (Andersen & Hill-Collins, 2006) and remains the foundation for systems of power and inequality. Race continues to structure our society in ways that value some lives more than others based on their race.

Race is important in any attempt to understand the complexities of reentry and IPV due to African Americans being disproportionately incarcerated in the U.S. and representing a larger number of formerly incarcerated individuals reentering society each year. Furthermore, the profile of men and women incarcerated who are subsequently released parallels the profile of couples who experience more lethal and severe forms of IPV. African Americans are more likely to be killed or to sustain serious injury because of intimate partner violence as Fagan (1996) and Rennison and Welchans (2000) have shown. Therefore, it is important to understand the role race plays in shaping reentry experiences.

Class is also pertinent to understanding the complexities of reentry and IPV. Like race, class shapes the opportunities, resources, and life chances of most black men and women. It restricts their access to employment, healthcare, education, and housing. Black men and women from the lower class lack the necessary resources, networks, and social capital that would increase their chances of reintegrating successfully. Their lives are powerfully shaped by class, and in order to understand their reentry experiences it is critical to understand the significance of belonging to such a highly marginalized group and how that marginalization influences the reentry experiences of male and female offenders.

As such, the overwhelming majority of individuals incarcerated in the U.S. come from the lower class. The criminal justice system in general, and the prisons in particular, have historically served as the principal arena for responding to the crimes of the lower class (Mauer, 1999). African Americans are disproportionately poor and crime victims also disproportionately represent the lower classes (Barak, Flavin, & Leighton, 2001).

Marc Mauer states:

> When we speak about race and the criminal justice system, we are often in fact also talking about class. How to untangle these overlapping effects is a complex problem, but one that is critical to understanding the status of African Americans and the criminal justice system (Mauer, 1999, p. 162).

Gender is also pertinent to understanding the complexities of reentry and IPV. Gender represents one of the major social statuses that determine the life chances of individuals. Like race and class, gender influences one's access to property, power, and prestige. In the United States, many females are subjected to inequality based mainly as a result of being born into the female group. During reentry, gender influences men and women's opportunities and access to programs and services differentially. More specifically, for women the resources and services available to address their unique needs are limited due in part to difference in male and female patterns of criminal offending.

In the criminal justice system, men and women are differentially affected by rate of imprisonment and ultimately, reentry as well. There are clear gender differences in criminal involvement. Men represent (93%) of the incarcerated population, while women represent seven percent (DeLisi & Conis, 2013). It follows that attention to gender identity as a broad influence on both behavior and opportunity must be incorporated into an understanding of what the men and women released from prison need in order to reintegrate successfully into their respective racial communities upon their release (Richie, 2001).

Due to the overwhelming proportion of men incarcerated within U.S. prisons, relatively little attention has been devoted to incarcerated women. The majority of studies conducted have focused extensively on men and the challenges such as employment, housing, and access healthcare that men encounter (Hairston & Oliver, 2006; Taylor-Greene et al., 2007; Visher & Travis, 2003; Solomon & Waul, 2001). Research is extremely limited in regards to the challenges women face during reentry, with the exception of a few precious studies (Richie, 2001; WPA, 2008). Research is even further limited in the area of reentry and IPV, with the studies of (Hairston & Oliver 2006; and Bobbitt, Campbell, & Tate, 2006) serving as the sole foundations upon which to build. It is known that violence affects men and women differently. The majority of intimate partner violence in the U.S. is perpetrated by men against women, as data reported by the Bureau of Justice Statistics (2006) indicate. It is crucial that gender be entered into the equation when discussing or attempting to understand the complexities of reentry and intimate partner violence.

In actuality, race, gender, and class all impact one's life chances. More specifically, race, gender, and class can either limit or serve as a catalyst to opportunities afforded to individuals. In the United States, women are treated differently from men in many respects. This is the same society with a rich history of racial inequality towards African Americans. In light of this, the opportunities for African American men and women who are returning to their communities are generally limited at best. Many of them have faced obstacles or have had limited economic opportunities prior to their felony convictions and are further alienated and ostracized, after returning home with such a conviction attached to their personhood. Many African American men and women return to home communities that are already struggling with high unemployment rates, poverty, and a general lack of resources. In the absence of resources and economic opportunities, they may become frustrated and ultimately some may even resort to violence towards the men and women who are "dearest" to them, their intimate partner.

Many formerly incarcerated individuals, including African American men and women, have extensive criminal histories and their backgrounds are often difficult to overcome (Delisi & Conis, 2010). During reentry the men and women come face- to- face with the reality of social rejection when they attempt to reconcile their lives. For some, they return home with high hopes and expectations to rebuild their lives. They soon realize that their conviction continues to play a part in the challenges they face, and for many they also realize their race and gender will further structure their post-incarceration experiences as well.

Although many desire to become productive, law-abiding citizens, in reality they are not afforded the same economic opportunities as a result of the negative stereotypes and perceptions associated with being a criminal-black-man or a criminal-black-woman (Rome, 2004). Black men and women understand the importance of *"restoring"* their lives, finding employment, securing housing, reuniting with children, and how central these factors are to the reentry process. In doing so, they recognize how race, gender, and class shape their experiences. Recent research acknowledges that race, gender, and class play a significant role in reentry challenges. As Pager (2007) has found, race plays a significant part in economic opportunities for African American men. This finding is important and suggests that something more may actually be happening in the lives of black men to explain the lack of opportunities afforded to African American men.

Many African American women face similar challenges to African American men during the reentry process. Finding employment and securing housing are challenges for many formerly incarcerated individuals reentering society, and many women lack the support that researchers have acknowledged plays a crucial role in reintegration. Social networks are important and play an essential role in formerly incarcerated individuals' successful transition from prison back into the community. Research has also found that strengthening the family network and maintaining supportive family contact can improve outcomes for both family members and prisoners (Sullivan et al., 2002). Likewise, most formerly incarcerated women believe that familial support is an important factor in helping them stay out of prison; however, for many African American women family ties have been severed as a result of the criminal behavior. In the absence of support and love from family, some women endure or tolerate men who are not so loving. In addition, many African American women with previous experiences of intimate partner violence at the hands of men are not passive victims. They may reciprocate such violence, and for some, become the perpetrators of such violence.

When faced with intimate partner violence and difficulties with reentry, many African Americans become frustrated and seek alternative ways to express their frustration. As a socially marginalized group, African American men and women are stigmatized, alienated, and closely scrutinized by society. Even though many formerly incarcerated individuals have served their time and hope to restore their lives and reintegrate successfully back into their respective communities, some will never have a "clean start." They carry with them the constant reminder of being a convicted felon, a label that continues to follow them throughout life.

In essence, many African American men and women who make great efforts to restore their lives are bombarded on different levels with not only the challenges associated with reentry, but also with forms of social oppression. Race, gender, and class factor into the reentry process and have specific implications for African Americans who are involved in intimate relationships and are trying to restore their lives. Many are at a crossroad, whereby race, gender, and class intersect and impact their opportunities, which ultimately, has the potential to negatively impact their intimate relationships. They experience what it is like to be poor- black- men and women and how those statuses intersect to shape their experiences of violence during reentry. In sum, the impact of incarceration and reentry on African American men, African American women, and the African American community is complex.

Victims: Intimate Partners

Restorative justice initiatives outline an approach to criminal behavior that explicitly acknowledges the victim. Such initiatives suggest that the justice system can be reformed to give effective "voice" to incarcerated African American men and women, who in many instances have been both the victim and offender in our criminal justice system. As victims of intimate partner violence, African Americans' shame and stigma prevent their access to assistance and often their willingness to be involved in a therapeutic or reparative process. African Americans often resist requesting support from formal systems of care, such as the criminal justice and social service systems (Bent-Goodley, 2001, 2003; Joseph, 1997; West, 1999; Garfield, 2005). Due to racial loyalty, "African American women may withstand abuse and make a conscious self-sacrifice for what she perceives as the greater good of the community, but to her own physical, psychological, and spiritual detriment" (Bent-Goodley, 2001, p. 323). Rather than share their stories, African American women tend to shield themselves from any form of public disclosure. For that reason, it is necessary that African American women be approached with sensitivity and respect. With intimate partner violence, victims are uniquely vulnerable to their intimate partner, the offender. Which approach, measures and techniques will or will not work with respect to their own safety should be considered with great care.

The voices of the victims should be heard, and they should be given a principal role in the process. The voice of the victim is essential to efforts that hold the offender accountable. In cases of IPV, the victim may have vital information about the offender's past, present, and potential behavior, therefore, victims' comments and insights may potentially shed light on the effort to develop successful strategies to manage offenders in the community. An important fact that must be recognized in reentry initiatives is that most offenders know their victims. Crime is often highly personal, and as with IPV it involves someone they know.

The Community: Disenfranchised

Communities should be able to provide offenders with the opportunity to show remorse, be held accountable, and live productive, crime-free lives. However, communities that receive high volumes of returning prisoners, as with many African American urban communities, are characterized by social and economic disadvantage, including high levels of unemployment, poverty, and high crime rates (Delisi & Conis 2010). In essence, many African American men and women are returning to communities with limited resources that are unable to provide adequate resources to their residents, and are not in a position to assist or address the multiple needs of formerly incarcerated men and women. Many offenders from historically oppressed minority communities rife with crime, poverty, and unemployment are themselves victims of historical inequalities (Conners, 2003).

Furthermore, Clear (2006) acknowledges that trying to restore individuals who have committed crimes to pre-crime levels when they reside in communities deprived of basic social infrastructure is unreasonable. Similarly, McCold (1996) challenges the reasonableness of successfully reintegrating an offender into a crime-ridden community as a productive and law abiding member of society without addressing the existing social structures. It is critical to recognize this dilemma when trying to develop strategies of restorative justice in extremely disadvantaged communities.

SIGNIFICANCE

This research compares African American men and women's experiences of intimate partner violence during the reentry process. It explores the ways in which race, gender, and class intersects to structure their experiences during that process. The intersection of race, gender, and class is useful as an analytical tool to aid in understanding the similarities as well as differences in their reentry experiences. This research is designed to document the personal perspectives and experiences of intimate partner violence by socially marginalized African Americans during the reentry process.

Four research questions guided this study:

1. What are the socioeconomic experiences of African American men and women during the reentry process?
2. How are their experiences similar and different?
3. What role does intimate partner violence play during the reentry process?
4. How are African American men and women's IPV experiences similar and different?

Summary

Every year in this country hundreds of thousands of African American men and women are released from prison back into their respective communities. Many are released into communities that are already overburdened with issues of unemployment, high crime rates, poverty, and limited resources. Not only are they returning to communities with limited resources, they are also confronting social inequalities as a result of their race, gender, and class. When examining the lives of formerly incarcerated African American men and women and their experiences of intimate partner violence during reentry, the intersecting role's of race, gender, and class must be addressed.

CHAPTER 2

The Process

INTERSECTIONALITY

A blended methodology that includes an intersectional and a comparative analytical framework was utilized in this study. The concept of intersectionality, first introduced by Kimberle Crenshaw (1991, 1993), is a tool for analyzing how various socially and culturally constructed categories intertwine. Cultural patterns of oppression are not only interrelated, but are bound together and influenced by the intersectional systems of oppression such as race, gender, and class (Hill-Collins, 2000). Intersectionality is utilized as a device to gain a better understanding of the various ways in which race, gender, and class intersect to shape formerly incarcerated individual's experiences of violence during the reentry process. It can be argued that many of the experiences faced by formerly incarcerated offenders cannot be fully understood by focusing solely on race, only at gender, or exclusively on class. Rather, it is necessary to consider analyzing these social factors simultaneously in order to get a complete understanding of their lived experience.

As such, a focus on the intersections of race, gender, and class only highlights the need to account for multiple grounds of identity when considering how social and cultural experiences are constructed (Crenshaw, 1991). Each individual has multiple identities and characteristics that affect and shape their life experiences. The interaction of characteristics such as race and gender provides each individual a perspective that influences how they view and experience the world. At any given moment, race, gender, and class may feel more salient or meaningful in a given person's life, but they are overlapping and cumulative in their effects in people's experiences (Anderson &

Hill-Collins, 1998, p.3). Intersectionality provides a framework to examine interrelating characteristics that requires more than simply performing separate analyses of race, gender, and class to understand the nature of one's experiences. Focusing on how race and gender frame the experiences of men and women creates opportunities for inquiry.

COMPARATIVE ANALYSIS

Additionally, it is not only important to understand how race and gender shape African American men's and women's experiences during reentry, but also to understand the differences, as well as similarities of their experiences during the reentry process. As a result, a comparative analysis is utilized. According to Ragin (1987), qualitative comparative analysis is well suited for addressing questions about outcomes resulting from multiple and conjectural causes where different conditions combine in different and sometimes contradictory ways to produce the same or similar outcomes. The focus is on comparing cases, which are examined in whole, as combinations of characteristics. The process of comparative analysis, therefore, allows researchers to continuously reshape and refine themes (Straus & Corbin, 1990). Comparative analysis strengthens the methodology by providing a tool to analyze the differences and similarities, especially with respect to gender during the reentry process. A comparative analysis of the formerly incarcerated African American men's and women's experiences was conducted by comparing and contrasting themes that emerged from the data to see what similarities and differences existed.

POPULATION AND SAMPLE

Participants in this study were recruited from the Fortune Society, a non-profit organization operating in Long Island City, New York. According to their mission statement, the Fortune Society is dedicated to strengthening the fabric of communities by promoting successful prisoner reentry and promoting alternatives to incarceration for offenders. The Fortune Society provides a range of connection to services such as housing, education, counseling, and other life-skills training programs to a historically underserved population, helping them become contributing members of society. Annually, Fortune Society serves approximately 3,000 men and women out of three New

York City area locations. This organization was selected not only because of their prisoner reentry program and services, but also due to their willingness to provide access to study participants as a result of its current affiliation with the John Jay College of Criminal Justice community.

In order to capture the complexities of the men and women's experiences, a multi- method research strategy was employed which included the use of 29 qualitative face-to-face interviews with formerly incarcerated African American men and women, ten Fortune Society staff interviews, and an examination of intake data for the period January 2008 to September 2011. Qualitative interviews were conducted with ten staff members to gain a better understanding of their perspective of intimate partner violence and the institutional response made during reentry. Both areas of data were triangulated to provide insights into the relationship between reentry and IPV. The use of multiple methods provides a means to triangulate data which is a common strategy utilized to increase confidence in the validity and reliability of qualitative analyses (Marshall & Rossman, 1989).

RECRUITMENT PROCESS

To participate in the study, staff members were required to have worked directly with or have knowledge of the experiences of formerly incarcerated individuals at Fortune Society. A description of the study was presented verbally to senior staff to gain access to the research site. A list containing contact information such as phone numbers and email addresses of employees was provided to the researcher. Letters were mailed and phone calls were made to potential subjects to inform them of the study. Formerly incarcerated subjects were required to be: an adult, self-identified as Black/African American male and females, served time in prison, and have/had been involved in a significant intimate relationship since release.

Several steps were utilized to recruit the formerly incarcerated African American study participants. Flyers were posted and distributed throughout the research site. Information about the research study was disseminated to potential subjects instructing them to contact the researcher if they were interested in the study. Staff members were also asked to spread the word about the study. After subjects agreed to participate in the study and met the limited criteria for participation, a date and time were set to conduct the interview. Fortune Society provided private office space for the interviews; as a result, 29 interviews were conducted at the research site.

CONFIDENTIALITY

This study was strictly voluntary and adhered to John Jay College's Institutional Review Board (IRB) standards and procedures for human subjects. Subjects were aware that they could discontinue participation at any time without penalty or loss of benefits to which the subject is otherwise entitled. After agreeing to participate in the study, an informed consent form was explained and signed as mandated by the IRB protocol. Participants were provided a copy of the consent form and were compensated with twenty-five dollars for their participation. Participants were given pseudonyms to ensure confidentiality. Records identifying the subject will remain confidential in perpetuity.

STAFF INTERVIEWS

All of the interviews with Fortune Society staff were recorded using a digital voice recorder. The interviews lasted between sixty and ninety minutes. The interview guide in Appendix A was designed to gain insight into staff members' perceptions of formerly incarcerated individual's experiences relating to reentry and intimate partner violence, and what institutional response was occasioned to address their needs. The objective in using an in-depth interview technique was to provide respondents with wide latitude in describing their perceptions of the challenges faced by formerly incarcerated African American men and women as they transitioned from prison to life back in the community.

Ten staff members were interviewed to learn from those who are intimately involved in the management and delivery of essential services for formerly incarcerated individuals about the pressing and important issues of prisoner reentry. The staff members interviewed held positions as a job developer, job readiness trainer, program assistant, family service attorney, family service counselor, social worker/clinical supervisor, employment coordinator, and group specialist. Interviews included questions such as: Do African American men and women experience intimate partner violence differently during the reentry process? Do you have a sense if violence is occurring in the lives of formerly incarcerated African American men and women? Staff interviews were conducted in the staff member's office or a private room at the research site. The interviews were semi-structured, with open-ended questions that allowed for probing. The interview data collected were later transcribed for detailed qualitative analysis. Detailed information was provided from the staff member's perspective of the experiences that formerly incarcerated African American men and women have in prison, the challenges they face once released, and their experiences of intimate partner violence.

When the interview was complete, participants were asked if they were to conduct a study such as this one, what questions would they of ask clients. During this time many provided at least two questions that should be considered. Half of the staff members were formerly incarcerated; therefore, the conversations provided them with the opportunity to think about their own lives, reflect on where they have been, and consider their own future. The interviews resulted in a rich contextual examination of the viewpoints of several staff members and from a formerly incarcerated person's viewpoint.

FORMERLY INCARCERATED CLIENTS' INTERVIEWS

The interviews with the formerly incarcerated were also semi-structured with open-ended questions that allowed for probing. The participants were first asked to share a little about themselves and their childhood experiences, followed by questions about their incarceration experiences. Participants provided detailed information about a typical day in prison, everyday violence, and the role of race and gender in their experiences. Questions were asked about the impact incarceration had on their own lives, and how imprisonment affected relationships with their families, friends, and intimate partners. Participants were also asked about their reentry experiences and whether or not they believed their race or gender shaped their experiences. Specific questions were then asked about the nature of their intimate relationships. Questions were posed regarding the length of their relationship, the individual with whom they were or had been involved, and whether or not the process of reentry created a source of conflict in their relationship. Participants were also asked if they had perpetrated violence or been a victim of IPV since release. The interview guide appears in Appendix B.

When the interview was complete, participants were asked to share their thoughts about the interview. During this sharing time many stated that the interview was therapeutic and helpful. The interview provided participants with the opportunity to think about their lives, reflect on where they have been, and consider what direction they wanted to go in the future. The in-depth interviews resulted in a rich contextual examination of the formerly incarcerated experiences while in prison, the reintegration challenges they faced once released, and their experiences of intimate partner violence during reentry. The interviews provided a unique opportunity to examine the context, circumstances, and events of their lives as once-incarcerated offenders now at liberty.

However, capturing detailed facets about formerly incarcerated men's and women's personal lives is not always a simple task. There are various reasons why formerly incarcerated individuals may be guarded about discussing the nature of their experiences and unlawful activities, including attempts to avoid shame and embarrassment, guilt, or even incrimination. This is especially relevant given that throughout the course of the interview study participants were asked to disclose rather private information about themselves and their families and associates. In order to build trust, familiarity, and rapport the interview began with rather innocuous questions such as demographic information followed by more sensitive questions about intimate partner violence. Participants were informed that this was a learning process and the objective was to learn from it. This preface to the interview provided them with a sense of empowerment in the research process as it allowed them the opportunity to be heard and have their own perspectives taken seriously.

Eliminating the actual influence of the researcher is nearly impossible; therefore the goal of the study was not to eliminate this influence, but to understand it and use it productively. The researcher acknowledges the benefits as well as the limitations of being the instrument of use for this study. The researcher's racial background, age, and doctoral training benefited the project in the ability to relate to the formerly incarcerated clients based on racial similarities, age cohort familiarity, and being able to interview participants with an understanding of the reentry process. On the other hand, as a college educated, law-abiding African American woman there was an understanding of how these factors could be potential obstacles in similar ways as the benefits. The life experiences of the researcher have most certainly shaped the lens employed for viewing certain situations, problems, and phenomena.

At the end of the interview, most of the men and women acknowledged that they felt comfortable speaking with the researcher and had a positive feeling about sharing their life experiences. Conversely, many of the women who were mothers felt uncomfortable with questions pertaining to their relationship with their children. As such, many of the women refrained from discussing details about their relationships or lack thereof, arguably due to the professional nature of the researcher alike. A few of the interviews were very emotional for the participant and the researcher. In one particular case, the participant was very emotional when discussing his childhood. The researcher had to stop the interview to allow the participant to gain control of his feelings. In a separate incident, the participant's account of the crime associated with her last conviction was very overwhelming for the researcher. As a result, the researcher cancelled other interviews arranged for that day.

INTAKE DATA

The Fortune Society provided access to intake data from January 2008 to September 2011, which was used to provide further statistical information that helps to contextualize the qualitative component of the research. The intake data collected included: program participant age, gender, race, housing, parental status, educational attainment, number of felonies, substance abuse.

ANALYSIS OF DATA: GROUNDED THEORY

The goal of understanding phenomena from the point of view of the participants and their particular social and institutional context is largely lost when textual data are quantified (Maxwell, 1996). Therefore, grounded theory, a qualitative approach, is utilized to collect, code, and analyze common themes present within individual accounts of their experiences and perceptions of intimate partner violence during reentry. With grounded theory, the focus of the analysis is organizing ideas and generating theory rather than collecting data to test existing theories (Glaser & Strauss, 1967).

The discovery of theory from data provides relevant predictions, explanations, and interpretations (Glaser & Strauss, 1967). Theory building is done by linking categories and different segments of data. Generating a theory from data means that most hypotheses and concepts not only come from the data, but are systematically worked out in relation to the data during the course of the research. In essence, no precisely defined hypotheses are formulated; instead, general aims and theoretical notions about the phenomenon being studied are tentatively formulated. Grounded theory enables the qualitative differences in the experiences of men and women during reentry to be captured. Specifically, it provides a theoretical framework for understanding the roles gender and violence play in shaping formerly incarcerated individuals' experiences during reentry.

The analysis is organized by themes that emerged from the data and includes an overview of their experiences and the role that race, gender, and class plays in shaping those experiences. The data collected were analyzed inductively for patterns regarding how participants interpreted and defined their personal experiences. The analysis of collected data began immediately after the first day of interviews and continued throughout the data collection process. The reading of the interview transcripts and observational notes then followed. The next step was open coding, which involved searching the data for emerging concepts and repeating themes. Once concepts and themes were identified, each transcription was reread to extract quotes that were used in writing up the results. The data were then separated into categories such as: challenges with reentry, sources of conflict between formerly incarcerated individuals and their partners, and experiences of intimate partner violence during reentry. Quotes and accounts of their experiences are utilized to provide a contextualized understanding to gain further insight into the experiences of study participants. Illustrative quotes were selected based upon the central issues and themes that emerged from the data.

A comparative analysis of the formerly incarcerated African American men's and women's experiences was conducted by comparing and contrasting themes that emerged from the data to see which similarities and which differences existed. Staff data were analyzed in the same manner as the data for the formerly incarcerated men and women, with the exception of a comparative analysis. Validation of the data was achieved through triangulation of methods by comparing staff members' perspectives, formerly incarcerated clients' perspectives, and intake data for Fortune Society over the period 2008-2011.

The narratives presented in this study are not simply participants' accounts of their experiences and actions to be assessed in terms of truth or falsity; rather, it is part of the reality that the researcher attempted to understand. The researcher is not conveying that the narratives represent the truth, nor is the veracity of their stories questioned. The narratives depict their social world and are based on their worldview. The researcher is interested in not only their experiences, but also in how participants make sense of these experiences and how their own individual understanding influences their behavior.

LIMITATIONS

Although this research strategy provides formerly incarcerated African American men and women with the opportunity to discuss their experiences of IPV during the reentry process, there are limitations of the study deserving of formal recognition. First, the study does not include a random sample, but rather reflects a convenience sample. Secondly, the sample is relatively small. The use of small samples in qualitative research provides in-depth understandings, appreciation, insights, and intimate familiarity (Roberts, 2003). Moreover, sample sizes are typically smaller in qualitative research because, as the study goes on, acquiring more data does not necessarily lead to more information. To account for the relatively small sample size, the mixed methods approach, specifically the intake data, supplemented the 29 in depth interviews.

Furthermore, characteristics of the formerly incarcerated men and women participants mirrored the characteristics of individuals incarcerated within our nation's prisons. Consequently, the findings reported are not suitable for the projection of broad generalizations. Despite these limitations, this study provides significant insight into the lives of formerly incarcerated African American men and African American women and their experiences of IPV within and against structures of race, gender, and class oppression. The results presented in this book, then, are important because they provide a starting point that future researchers may use to examine the role race, class, and gender play in shaping men's and women's experiences of IPV during reentry.

Summary

In order to capture the complexities of the experiences of formerly incarcerated African American men and women, a multi- method research strategy was employed. Together these processes were designed to enhance theoretical sensitivity, reduce researcher bias, minimize traditional patterns of thinking, and avoid over-reliance on common knowledge derived from past experiences and literature (Strauss & Corbin, 1990). The utilization of an emergent qualitative design allowed for rigorous examination of the in-depth interviews which proved useful toward an understanding of African American men's and women's experiences during reentry.

CHAPTER 3

Inside Look From the Outside

STAFF

The Fortune Society organization employs over 190 employees; over 80% of their staff members are people of color. The vast majority (70%) are formerly incarcerated and/or have histories of substance abuse or homelessness. The organization's leadership believes strongly in the concept of peer support; consequently, they actively recruit staff with this particular life experience. Formerly incarcerated staff members are in a position to help their clients address the often multiple and frequently competing challenges of reentry.

For this study, ten staff members were interviewed to learn from those who are involved in the management and delivery of essential services for formerly incarcerated individuals. Staff members were interviewed to gain insight into the challenges that formerly incarcerated African American men and women experience during reentry. More specifically, staff interviews were designed to determine if intimate partner violence occurs in the lives of formerly incarcerated African American men and women, and if so how it is addressed by the organization.

Of the ten staff members interviewed six identified themselves as African American; four males and two females made up the group of ten. Four staff members identified as White, and all four of them were women. Six out of the ten staff members were formerly incarcerated. Staff members interviewed held positions such as a job developer, job readiness trainer, program assistant, family service attorney, family service counselor, social worker/clinical supervisor, employment coordinator, and group specialist.

Organization of Staff Data

Staff interviews produced several important themes- those being challenges during reentry, issues of reentry and intimate partner violence, and barriers in addressing the needs of African American men and women during reentry. The following sections provide detailed accounts of the staff's perspectives with respect to these three themes.

Challenges During Reentry

Staff members acknowledged that formerly incarcerated men and women typically face multiple challenges when reentering society. A general consensus exists that the most pressing and pertinent issues for men and women returning are finding and maintaining employment, suitable housing, and negotiating relationships. Although the majority of staff members agreed that housing is an important issue, they did not discuss the issue of housing in any great detail. Moreover, negotiating relationships is addressed in the reentry and intimate partner violence section. Accordingly, the following section provides detailed accounts of staff members' perspectives on the challenges associated with finding and maintaining employment and a brief discussion of housing challenges. In sharing their perspectives, several staff members related how race, gender, and class tend to shape the experiences of formerly incarcerated African American men and women.

<u>Employment</u>

Finding and maintaining employment is considered by staff members as essential for reintegration. The majority of staff acknowledged that most of the men and the women returning from prison lack a high school diploma, are deficient in basic skills, and lack the necessary experience for well-compensated jobs. Raymond, a job developer in charge of assisting clients in securing employment, discussed some detail a range of challenges faced by formerly incarcerated men and women. He explains that he often assists individuals who have been incarcerated since a very young age; their education is commonly very limited. Raymond emphasizes that "it can be challenging" when trying to develop and prepare individuals to "go out and sell themselves in society" when their educational foundation is so limited.   He acknowledges that, "people just have a lack of self-confidence about themselves because of their past experiences and we try to bring that out of them."

Pamela, a soft skills trainer, refers to herself as the "Miss Manners of the felon world." Pamela is responsible for preparing clients for jobs, assisting them with adjusting their attitude and behavior, and preparing them for job interviews. She acknowledges that the two main challenges for formerly incarcerated men and women are employment and housing. She describes what it is like for men and women with prison backgrounds reintegrating back into society. Pamela's remarks highlight the complexities associated with reentry, as she reveals:

> There are a lot of seams in the transition from coming out of prison and getting back into society as a functioning member…Once they come out they hit a lot of potholes. Such things as lack of recent job history, lack of marketable skills, lack of stable living environment. Even if you tell them OK, well we have a stable living environment for them that's still not going to help that fact that they haven't worked in the past fifteen years.

Pamela goes on to explain:

> Now I put you in transitional housing and for lack of a better term it's kind of a shit hole. You are sharing a room with six other gentlemen, gentlemen I am using loosely. Sometimes they are there for the same reason as you are, sometimes they are looking for a flop house. Sometimes you get your stuff stolen, sometimes you don't. Sometimes some of these places are not the most hygienic place in the whole world. They are not the Hilton. Now you are kind of trapped off there. How do you get out of that environment? You have to get a job. OK, well your job is not paying enough for you to pay rent. By the way, you owe X amount of dollars in child support too…its a burden for someone who is working minimum wage… most of these guys' skill sets don't really dictate much more than $9 an hour maybe. These are some of the things they run into…those are some of the gaps.

Barbara, a program assistant, is responsible for interviewing, assessing, and evaluating clients' progress while participating in services rendered by the Fortune Society organization. She points out that the social stigma associated to being a convicted felon is a problem for many:

> I think part of the problem is the stigma that is attached to the people who come out…society just assumes that everybody that has been incarcerated is a screw up and a danger to the world…As someone who was formerly incarcerated you feel like it is tattooed on your forehead felon that everybody can see.

Many formerly incarcerated men and women lack the necessary skills and education to obtain a job; however, Raymond, a job developer, insists that inequalities exist in regards to employment opportunities during reentry. In the words of Raymond:

> It is easier for a woman to get employed that's been incarcerated than a man in my opinion. Black men can be seen as a threat. I think that it's all around the board. Employers are more likely to give a woman a shot before they give it to a black man.

Raymond's account demonstrates possible inequalities that are occurring during reentry. Critical race theorists argue that racial inequality is the normal way of doing business in U.S. society. When asked why he believed this is happening, Raymond candidly replied, "well they have a conviction or convictions, plus they are black men." In essence, Raymond acknowledges that the bias associated with black men not being able to obtain employment could be a result of their multiple convictions and the mere fact that they are black men acting in deadly combination.

<u>Housing</u>

As previously outlined, staff members acknowledged that securing appropriate affordable housing is an issue for many formerly incarcerated men and women alike; however, they did not provide extensive comments in reference to housing. In her previous comments,

Pamela mentions that "transitional housing and for lack of a better term it's kind of a shit hole"- however, men and women that are lacking resources and do not have other housing options generally rely on shelters and temporary housing for a place to stay. Ava, a job developer, in charge of assisting clients in finding employment, stated the following in this regard: 'housing is the biggest thing…people need a stable place to live." She discussed the problems with temporary housing, more specifically boarding house accommodations and explains, "If I am just coming from prison this room could remind me of a cell. People don't think about that. They are opening up these three-quarter houses and they look like dorms in prison." She acknowledges that for some women they feel like they are back in prison because of "staying in a room with six other people" and are sleeping "on a bunk bed." Ava explains that women often state that "I could have stayed in jail for this." Barbara, a program assistant, also describes some additional complexities associated with reentry housing:

> Housing is horrible when you have been incarcerated no matter how long ago. Landlords aren't supposed to turn you down but they do. They just turn you away. They say your credit is not good enough. Housing is a tough one. This is a bad economy and right now it's incredibly difficult for anyone to get a foot in, let alone someone who has already got a felony on their record.

Issues of Reentry & Intimate Partner Violence

Nearly half of the staff members confirmed that intimate partner violence occurs in the lives of formerly incarcerated African American men and women during their reentry. Staff members provided detailed accounts of incidents and occurrences; in doing so they provided several explanations as to why they believe IPV often takes place in the lives of African American men and women. Jessica, the family service attorney at the Fortune Society, who is responsible for assisting clients with obtaining custody or visitation privileges with their children, family offense petitions which involves orders of protection, and child support, shares her own perspective. She notes that "sometimes they will tell you about it." She further noted:

> If there is a history I always hear about the history [referring to history of intimate partner violence]. It takes a while because they don't want to sour our relationship straight away. I try to bring it up a lot because it helps court cases. I work differently with the clients than the other staff does. I'm not a counselor. I don't care about your feelings. I do, but I want to work on with what's relevant to the court case. If DV [domestic violence] is going on you have to tell me and we have to deal with it or its going to screw you.

Jessica admits that clients generally have been forthcoming about their experiences of intimate partner violence:

> I have had guys tell me that they have hit their girlfriends, "Yeah I slapped her once. Or she attacked me first or she knew that if she hit me she knew the cops would come and arrest me." It's one of those types of things and I would say its self defense.

Pamela, a soft skills trainer, insists adamantly that, "we see it a lot." She acknowledges that she sees guys who "Get caught up in domestic violence cases and end up going back and forth to Rikers Island." Pamela also described one particular incident in considerable detail.

> Recently we had a woman here. She was trying to better her station in life. By coming here she wanted to get herself a job. She had a great personality. She was coming along well with the interviewing skills. The baby's father at home suddenly started sabotaging her coming in. He would make her late in the morning. He would call her up two hundred times during the classroom hours, just trying to disrupt her and get her not to focus. He used to yell at her, "You don't need that place!"

Pamela goes on to explain that the boyfriend was afraid his girlfriend would realize that he is not providing her the support she needs. She continues:

> At first it was mental and it became physical to the point where he punched her in her eye. I saw her couple of weeks ago with a black eye. Yet and still she stays with him… why? She sees herself in the situation she is in and she doesn't believe she can command better; low self-esteem, low self-worth, it plagues people.

Rachel, an employment coordinator, responsible for placing clients in subsidized internships and conducting mock interviews, also confirms that intimate partner violence occurs in the lives of many African American men and women during their reentry. Rachel emphasizes, "Yes, definitely. There are so many times where somebody walks in here with a black eye, or cuts and bruises or we just don't see them and we don't know why we don't see them:"

> I think a lot of people are not forthcoming about it at all. They are sort of hiding it, may be trying to deal with it on their own. There are some women who I think they kind of feel like, "I am going to handle this. I am going to handle my own." In some ways maybe the violence goes both ways and it becomes more complicated in some ways.

To a greater extent than other groups, many African American women resist requesting support from formal systems of care and attempt to handle or deal with intimate partner violence on their own, as Garfield (2005) and Bent-Goodley (2001) have shown in their research. Rachel's account reveals that during reentry as well, African American women often resist seeking out support from formal systems.

One of the programs available at the Fortune Society organization that attempts to address the issues of intimate partner violence for men is an anger management program. Dennis, a counselor at the organization in charge of the anger management class, recalls a conversation with one of his clients in regards to dealing with violence perpetrated by the intimate partner:

> A lot of times I hear, 'I just ignore it.' There is some stuff you can't ignore, kind of raised a red flag for me. You are telling me you are so cool now that you just ignore it? But you have

been angry all this time? I can see it in groups that you have been angry and you were able to go home and ignore your wife? I find it a little difficult to believe. There is a human part of all of us that causes us to sometimes go above the level of anger that we really want to. I think they have a hard time dealing with that intimacy.

Staff members' accounts provided insight into the complexities of how men and women are experiencing IPV and how it influences their overall reentry experiences. Intimate partner violence plays a major part in individual court proceedings regarding visitation and orders of protection. On another level, intimate partner violence influences the level of commitment formerly incarcerated men and women may have to reentry programming- for example, job training, employment services, and anger management. In essence, based on staff members' accounts, intimate partner violence exacerbates the difficulties and challenges faced by many African American men and women engaged in the reentry process.

<u>Race and Intimate Partner Violence</u>

When asked if race plays a part in men's and women's experiences of intimate partner violence, nearly half of staff members agreed that race does matter. Rena, an African American, social worker and clinical supervisor at Fortune, is responsible for evaluating and assessing clients' needs. She shares her perspective in the following terms: "There is certainly a commonality with other races." However, she argues that there are some things that have been culturally accepted and considered "okay in the African American community." Rena explains how culturally African American families do not generally discuss violence within the household:

Whatever goes on in here stays in here. That is the cultural thing. As children, as people, we say it is not to be discussed. We are not supposed to cry and the emotions are not supposed to be there. I do think it's a direct and it's generational that it continues to happen and happen and happen…and when will we begin to say that it's not okay? When is that going to happen?

As Rena goes on to explain:

> There is certainly a cultural difference in how people deal with
> and define having been incarcerated. They may have to deal
> with certain prejudices just being incarcerated and being an
> African American. I think that what it does it creates far more
> of a sensitivity of how they reintegrate and deal with society
> as a whole when they are released.

Rena acknowledges that the inequalities that African American women encounter while incarcerated impact how they reintegrate into society once released. Similarly, Jessica, a family service attorney at the Fortune Society, argues that race does demonstrably impact experiences of IPV:

> I think so. I think culturally, in different cultures, it's more
> acceptable. I almost feel like it's…I don't want to say a more
> realistic view, the African American folks I have come across
> realize that it is wrong…it's not an acceptable behavior.
> Everyone gets caught in this circle and continue to endure it
> and don't know how to get out of it. I think there is a culture
> difference.

Rachel, an employment coordinator, and Pamela, a soft skills trainer, also expressed similar sentiments regarding race and intimate partner violence. The majority of clients seeking services at the Fortune Society are African American. Rachel believes that with the African American population, "it is often normalized." She contends, "Based on what I see it sometimes is more normalized. I don't know if it has to do so much with race, as much as the socio-economic status. We do see a lot of this, normalizing of it." Similarly, Pamela believes, based on the foregoing, the following:

> Based solely on observation, I don't have any stats to back this
> up, it seems to me that it is more frequent among African
> American men than the other races that I have come in contact
> with, men and women…the majority of the population that
> come through here are African American men that could

> definitely have something to do with it…A lot more of it is out
> of fear or desperation and lashing rather than being just a
> violent natured person. I think it's frustration, fear, and not
> having any other place to go with the emotions and
> aggressions.

Overall, the staff members acknowledged that race plays a role in shaping the experiences of intimate partner violence during reentry. They argued that for African Americans, particularly African American men, intimate partner violence is normalized, to a certain degree. Although African American men and women experience IPV often, their experiences and responses to such violence by no means equates to an acceptance of IPV as a part of life or as a normal event.

Staff members also contend that cultural differences by-and-large account for the disproportionate amount of violence experienced by African Americans.

<u>Gender & Intimate Partner Violence</u>

Although the majority of the staff did not comment extensively about gender and intimate partner violence, a few briefly discussed how they feel gender shapes the experiences of IPV.   They agreed that differences exist between men's and women's experiences of intimate partner violence during reentry. Additionally, the staff said that violence, to a certain degree, is related and could possibly be attributed to the violence in prison experiences. Recent literature acknowledges that men's prisons are more violent in comparison to women's prisons experiences (Clear et al., 2012). Barbara, a program assistant, argues that while incarcerated, "men deal with a much higher rate of violence on a day- to-day basis and men's facilities are much more volatile." On the other hand, Barbara believes, "women are more emotional creatures:"

> Women are going to argue, they are going to yell…but almost
> for a woman it is a last resort to actually put your hands on
> each other. For men coming out they have gotten inured. It has
> been normal for them. For them it has become more, I don't
> want to say acceptable, it's not acceptable, but normalized.
> Where a woman is going to argue and yell and men don't do

that so men hit each other. A man would turn around and smack a female and shut her up because that's what they do. It's not right. It's like you get programmed to deal with things in a certain manner. There needs to be like a reprogramming process.

Similarly, Rachel, an employment coordinator, observes the following in this regard: "I think there is some psychological trauma that can occur inside. Depending on the person, how long they were in." She asserts that the general atmosphere, especially inside men's prisons, "is based on fear…based on who is going to be the most macho and that's for their own protection." That fear, "can manifest itself in a lot of different ways." Rachel explains what may be happening:

> Well one thing that I personally see is that it has become so normalized and downplayed in the culture that I don't know if is taken as seriously as maybe it should be. It's such a commonplace event and I also think of course with this population, we are dealing with people that may have themselves been victims while they were inside and they may be just channeling that to the people that are closest to them, their girlfriend or boyfriend.

Conversely, James, a job readiness trainer in the Fortune Society organization, is responsible for preparing clients for jobs, assisting them with adjusting their attitude and behavior, and preparing them for job interviews. He observed that "most women that come from prison are more aggressive. I don't see them backing down and just accepting anything."

<u>Inability to Resolve Conflicts</u>

Over half of the staff members believed the violence experienced by many formerly incarcerated African American men and women in their intimate relationships is due to their lack of ability to resolve conflicts through discussion and compromise. The overwhelming majority of staff confirmed that conflict management is definitely an issue. Barbara, a program assistant, describes what may be happening:

> One of the biggest problems is one partner gets used to doing on their own and the other partner is trying to be controlling. They are trying to control someone that has lived however many months or years without that control. There is automatically conflict. Usually, hopefully, one or both have changed some over time so they are not the same people they expect when they get out. That causes more conflict, especially if you have been incarcerated for a long time. Sometimes the only way you know how to deal with things is through violence. They haven't learned other coping skills because that's the only way they know.

While men are incarcerated, their female partners have a tendency to stay around and support them during their incarceration. In stark contrast, the intimate partners of women often end the relationship. Consequently, this can play a part in the difference in the expression of intimate partner violence for formerly incarcerated men and women. Research has shown that intimate partner violence often starts with emotional violence, and then progresses to physical violence (CDC, 2012). Since men are more likely to return to an existing relationship, arguably they are more likely to experience more severe forms of intimate partner violence in their relationships as opposed to women who are involved in relatively new intimate relationships.

Barbara also explains how class shapes the experiences of intimate partner violence during reentry. She states in this regard:

> A lot of people resort to violence when they get afraid, when they get anxious, when they get nervous and when they don't know what else to do. All of those feelings and all of those overwhelming sensations happen when you first come out. If you don't know how to deal with them and you don't have the money or the ability to find a therapist or someone to listen to you, you turn to violence to find a way of getting rid of the things you don't want to deal with.

Barbara's narrative sheds light toward the role of class status during reentry. More specifically, in the absence of resources, formerly incarcerated individuals have to deal with their feelings and emotions based on the limited coping mechanisms and skills they already possess. Often, the ways in which many formerly incarcerated men and women deal with fear and anxiety is not the most effective way.

Jessica, a family service attorney, shared her perspective with enthusiasm. In the absence of conflict resolution skills, Jessica describes how partners often make use of orders of protection:

> People don't know how to resolve disputes. I can't believe the stuff I hear clients talking about. She looked at me funny so I stepped to her. I smacked her…it's like acceptable in some of the cultures where it's okay to beat the tar out of each other… I don't know if people don't have the skills or weren't brought up with the skills to resolve conflicts. It's crazy how things escalate into violence.

Jessica gives examples of how partners use orders of protection excessively:

> The last couple of cases I have worked on have involved orders of protection. I have had folks who just aren't violent with each other, but have long histories of orders of protection against everybody. They will have three of four partners where they have orders of protection and a history of DV (domestic violence) on both sides…It's sort of like these people…they beat the tar out of each other. It happens all the time. Folks use these orders of protection as a weapon… People call the police at the drop of a hat…I would love to think that women don't use this as a weapon, but they do and they are totally aware of it. It's amazing. The cops come, the cops arrest everybody, or the cops arrest the guys. And you can get orders of protection, simple, simple, simple.

Jessica also emphasizes that child support is a huge problem for men during reentry, and that consequently creates conflict within many relationships. She contends:

> When these guys get out they owe a tremendous amount of money. They think they have to pay in order to see their kids or the state is taking money directly out of their checks. They

aren't able to become part of the mainstream economy. So they can never actually get legitimate jobs with legitimate health insurance. You can't become a part of real society when you owe fifty thousand dollars and the second you make $500 part of it goes straight to the government to pay off child support.

Rena, a social worker and clinical supervisor at Fortune, acknowledges that, "there is a lot of depression in recently released clients when they can't assimilate as quickly. Self-esteem kind of fits in there as well. These are some of the things that I am finding when I do my psycho socials." Rena further explains that "depression and self-esteem, speak directly to why there are some difficulties connected to IPV." She states in this regard, "having lost a great deal of their lives and they have the tendency to turn that particular part of anger on their partners." Rena informed the researcher earlier in the interview that when conducting clinical assessments with formerly incarcerated men and women that served extended periods of time, often she did not witness their anger during their encounters; however, she acknowledges "the anger, it kind of manifests itself in relationships as opposed to society or just the anger of incarceration kind of leads to DV [domestic violence] and violence in the home." In other words, the men and women when interviewed for their assessments did not exhibit signs of anger; however, their anger was later displaced toward their intimate partners behind closed doors.

Rena also contends that the lack of preparation during release can create conflict for men and women alike. She explains:

It can lead to frustration and perhaps where a formerly incarcerated person may not have impulsive reactions outside the home that is something that may be repressed and can manifest itself in the home with family members. I think we kind of set them up for situations where it can lead to DV and certainly with the most vulnerable of clients that may have gone into the system with certain vulnerabilities anyway.

Similarly, Pamela, a soft skills trainer, believes that intimate partner violence is a form of control. More specifically, Pamela acknowledges fear of rejection when their partner tells them they are ending the relationship because they have had enough results in an ensuing conflict. As she states:

> Finally the girl gets fed up with the lifestyle that the guy is living. Rather than change, he is scared to death maybe I can't do anything else but this. Now he gets mad. He doesn't get mad at himself; maybe he is mad at himself but doesn't show it to himself instead he will lash out at the people closest to him... I believe its all fear based...I don't think these guys are bad guys. I think that they just don't know better....they don't realize its fear based.

James, a job readiness trainer, and Rachel, an employment coordinator, expressed similar thoughts as articulated by Pamela. James states, "when I look at the whole reentry violence thing it's a lot because people get confused and people are afraid to tell, even their lady." Rachel contends, "most importantly, the formerly incarcerated individual must first and foremost actually acknowledge that there is something wrong with it [intimate partner violence]. That it is not normal." She asserts that formerly incarcerated individuals are not taking responsibility for their actions. She states, "even if it's not physical violence, the power and control that is asserted over somebody, that is probably even harder for someone to take responsibility for and acknowledge." James, a job developer, acknowledges that the difficulties for some men and the conflict that ensues is based on not being able to be a provider:

> It's difficult for some men to come out here and have to see that their woman is the breadwinner now. She is the one that is standing on her feet. You got to settle for less, just not having enough to chip in or anything of that nature. Not being able to assist with the rent, assist with this. Women can play a part in it too. They start...look at [my] phone bill, look at my this, look at my that. Those little my's play a hazardous role in some guys performance in the way they act because they are already insecure about the fact that they are not the breadwinner. Sometimes it's hard to take a back seat.

Dennis, a counselor at Fortune, shares a conversation held with one of the men participating in his anger management class.

> I have had clients tell me on several occasions, "You know what I was thinking about when she was acting up?" You telling me that you are not in control? You are not. She is not property. Women are not your property.

BARRIERS IN ADDRESSING CLIENTS' NEEDS

Several staff members discussed the typical barriers associated with addressing the needs of formerly incarcerated African American men and women's experiences of intimate partner violence. Pamela, a soft skills trainer, commented on the attitude of the individual. She acknowledged, "we [Fortune] can only take it as far as the individual will let us." The majority of the staff members discussed some barriers perceived to exist at the organizational level in addressing clients' needs. Jessica, a family service attorney, contends:

> I think part of it is open-mindedness on the part of the clients. I think part of it is the way that you are raised that it's okay to behave in a certain manner. They see some of the programs that we are trying to administer as other, that's the "other" that's not how we do it where I am from. It's funny because as a white woman I teach a couple of classes. They are like, "Yo Jessica what do you have on your iphone? Don't you have Nickel back on your iphone? But it's stupid shit like that, or white girls they won't hit you back that kind of stuff. It's weird crazy preconceived notions.

In seeking clarification, Jaime was asked if she believes intimate partner violence was a "cultural issue" as she responds:

> If you want to say cultural like different neighborhoods or different ethnicity yeah sure. I have to say it is… I think open-mindedness is a part of it and I also think that you are coming from a place where it is completely acceptable and you are able to function in a place that it's completely acceptable.

Dennis, a counselor, also discussed some of the barriers in addressing their needs:

> A lot of it is socio-cultural…we are almost socialized to behave in a certain manner. Without the educational component that could possibly change the direction of the thought process people just continue to repeat the process… Well you are a man you are not supposed to cry. You are supposed to be in charge. Women are supposed to be domesticated.

Rena, a social worker and clinical supervisor at Fortune, contends that, "there needs to be more programming that's involved in trying to prepare an inmate for release back into society." She also argues that formerly incarcerated offenders who are still under correctional supervision, by means of probation or parole, should be mandated to particular programs such as anger management. She believes that having that connection to have the clients "kind of self-check in and say hey I didn't realize that. I didn't know I was doing these things" can prove beneficial. She further explains that when formerly incarcerated African American men and women don't know how to quell anger, "it can lead to being incarcerated again. It's very easy to do things behind closed doors as opposed to out in the open where there is the possibility of re-arrest."

The Fortune Society organization offers two programs that vaguely address the broad issues of domestic violence. Dennis, one of the counselors, explains:

> I am a family service counselor. I facilitate groups in the nature of domestic violence, but we use a different acronym for it… we use men's conflict resolution. Sometimes the clients are not able to understand the domestic violence part, so we give it a different name so that way it's easier for them to absorb.

Dennis acknowledges that there are two programs to deal with issues of domestic violence which includes men's conflict resolution, also referred to as anger management and healthy relationships. When asked about services or programs that address intimate partner violence the majority of staff mentioned the anger management program. Yet, several staff members tend to question the effectiveness of the program. Rachel, an employment coordinator at Fortune, expressed her doubts with respect to offering anger management programs to deal with intimate partner violence.

> You do not address domestic violence with anger management because it is not an anger management issue. Anger management tells you that you are entitled to your feelings and you just have to express them in a different way, but when it comes to a domestic violence relationship you are not entitled to tell somebody what to do. You are not entitled to hurt someone. Your feelings are irrational, misguided, and misplaced...

Similarly, Jessica, one of the family attorneys at Fortune, questioned the effectiveness of the anger management class also in the following terms:

> I see these guys that go through the anger management program and they still get mad, and they still get sweaty, and they still get freaked out when they talk about their girlfriends because everybody is trying to fuck each other over. No one wants to see the middle ground. It's about being right more so than doing the right thing.

Barbara, a program assistant in charge of assessing and evaluating clients' progress, expressed her concern with the anger management class as well. Her statements shed light on the barriers in addressing needs, specifically intimate partner violence in the lives of African American men and women during reentry. She shared the following:

> We do have anger management classes. I believe that our anger management and our family services actually need to have more focus on domestic violence issues. They are touched on, but they are not focused on it. Sometimes I think Fortune is like the whole world. If I don't open my eyes to it then it doesn't happen. Partners who are being abused tend to

cover it, tend to hide it so people don't see it. That is part of the nature of it until it is too late…What goes on outside of here sometimes isn't addressed. That's a problem. If you recognize it, then you have to do something about it. I don't think we are really qualified to do anything, so blinders sometimes…

Even Dennis acknowledges that intimate partner violence is occurring in the lives of the men whom he counsels in his men's resolution/anger management class. When asked how he deals with it, he responds, "Once you have knowledge of something you are responsible. Once you get the information, whatever you do with it is on you after that."

Jessica, the family service attorney, admits that her way of dealing with clients that are perpetrators of intimate partner violence is "to give my own little lectures to the guys." Several staff members acknowledge that they refer outside of the agency for services related to intimate partner violence. Pamela, a soft skills trainer, explains:

Occasionally we will get someone that comes through and we usually make the necessary referrals, recommend that they leave the spouse, but that's easier said then done. They want to go down with the ship, "Oh but I love so and so!" Well, you can love someone that doesn't beat the shit out of you.

When asked how the clients deal with intimate partner violence that occurs, Pamela responds:

They may talk about it a little bit, that's about it. Or totally try to just brush it off or hide it. They will come in visibly upset, but they will go into the bathroom and they won't want to talk about it. Maybe we will get them talking about it….if you are asking if they want to press charges or do they want to do something like that, absolutely not! I have never once seen that as an option, not that it's not offered up as an option, because we have to cover all bases, but that is usually never taken. Usually what they want to do is that they want to go home, talk it out, and fix it when in reality it is deeper.

Staff accounts thus revealed that African American men and women often perpetrate and are victims of intimate partner violence during reentry. Furthermore, staff members acknowledged that IPV is a problem. Even though staff members agreed they could likely play a more substantial role in addressing intimate partner violence, it was not viewed as a priority of the organization. For example, staff members cited referrals to other agencies and an ineffective anger management program to address men's issues of violence as a solution to dealing with intimate partner violence that occurs in the lives of formerly incarcerated men and women.

CHAPTER 4

More Than a Number: Unveiling the Mask

INTAKE DATA

The intake data utilized in this study is based on self-reports from clients recorded during their intake interview. Criminal data reported by clients is verified through a background check. Information provided by clients who are referred by the courts is cross-checked with court documents as well. The Data Systems department at the Fortune Society updates and maintains the client data. The department recently switched to a new web-based database to collect this type of data. Based on the intake data from January 2008 to September 2011, a general profile of the clients that the Fortune Society serves was captured. The intake data included a total of 6,667 clients. Of those clients, the vast majority (87%) were men, while women accounted for 13% of the clients. The overwhelming majority of clients (4, 378) were African American, representing roughly 66% of the total intake population. Of the 4, 378 African Americans, 3,726 or 85% were black men and 647 or 15% were black women. African American men and women represented, by far, the largest group of clients seeking services at the Fortune Society. Clients' ages range between 18 and 77. The majority of clients, 60% reported having children. As for educational attainment, 78% had eleven years of school or less. Sixteen percent of the clients were homeless. Over 78% reported that they did not have mental health concerns. Intake data did not include specific types of crime in a data field, only a progress note; however, that particular information was not included in the data provided to the researcher.

PROFILE OF STUDY PARTICIPANTS

Twenty-nine men and women met the limited criteria of being an adult, self-identified as Black/African American male or female, served time in prison, and have/had been involved in a significant relationship since release. Based on self-identified social characteristics generated from a semi-structured interview guide, a general profile of the selected participants revealed the following personal descriptions. Seventeen participants were men and 12 were women. The men range in age from 18 to 61 years old, while the women range in age from 22 to 51 years old. The overwhelming majority, 26, were born and raised in the New York City. Only one of the men was currently married, while three were divorced, and 13 have never been married. Only one woman was currently married, one separated, and ten of the women have never been married. Thirteen of the 17 men had children, and eight of the 12 women had children. All of the men identified their sexual orientation as heterosexual. Three of the women identified themselves as homosexuals.

Education

In terms of educational attainment, one man had earned a Bachelor's degree, three had obtained a Graduate Equivalency Diploma (GED), and 13 had dropped out of high school. Three women earned a Bachelor's degree, one earned an Associate's degree, two earned a high school diploma, and six dropped out of high school. Two of the women are actively pursuing a Master's degree, and one woman is in the process of completing the requirements for a bachelor's degree.

Employment

The majority of men and women were unemployed. Twenty of the 29 men and women were unemployed. Eleven of the 17 men were unemployed. The six men who were employed held jobs as a teacher, barber, chef, job trainer, career developer, and group coordinator. Four of the six men were employed by Fortune Society. Several participants indicated that they had never worked an "honest day in their life." The majority of women, nine, were unemployed. Two of the three women who were employed held jobs as a case manager and job trainer at

Fortune Society. The third woman who was employed worked at a correctional institution.

Although the majority of participants were unemployed at the time of the interview, finding a job was a top priority. The majority of unemployed participants were participating in job training and career development courses offered by the Fortune Society. Six of the eight men and women who were employed at the time of the interview worked for Fortune. They had completed programs at Fortune and were later hired.

Criminal History

For most study participants, their previous prison term was not their first encounter with the criminal justice system. Many participants began their criminal careers at quite a young age. Involvement with gangs was a contributing factor in participants' criminal careers, especially men. Eight of the 17 men reported they were a member of a gang prior to, during, or after their incarceration. None of the women reported being a member of a gang prior to, during, or after their incarceration.

All of the men reported having more than one conviction. Ten of the seventeen men reported having three or more felony convictions, and they had all served a prior prison term. With regard to their most recent conviction offense, male participants indicated a mix of crime types. Six of the men were drug offenders convicted of either dealing or possession, six were convicted of a violent offense (homicide, burglary, aggravated assault, robbery), three were convicted of a property offense, one was convicted for conspiracy, and one for possession of a weapon. The majority of men, nine of them, served one to five years for their last conviction.

Ten of the 12 women reported having more than one felony conviction. Three women reported having three or more felony convictions and had served a prior prison term. With regard to their most recent conviction offense, female participants indicated a mix of crime types. Three were drug offenders convicted of either dealing or possession, seven were convicted of a violent offense (homicide, burglary, aggravated assault, robbery), one was convicted of a property offense, and one was convicted for conspiracy. The overwhelming majority, eleven women served one to five years for their last conviction. Only one woman served more than five years in prison, having served 20 years for manslaughter and attempted murder.

Institutions

All of the men and women had served time in either medium or maximum security facilities. The men served time in several maximum security facilities, including Attica Correctional facility, Auburn Correctional Facility, Clinton Correctional Facility, Eastern New York Correctional Facility, Elmira Correctional facility, Great Meadow Correctional Facility, Green Haven Correctional Facility, Sing Sing Correctional Facility, and Upstate Correctional Facility. Several men were housed in medium security facilities, including Fishkill Correctional Facility, Gowanda Correctional Facility, Greene Correctional Facility, Hudson Correctional Facility, Otisville Correctional Facility, and Ulster Correctional Facility. Women served time in several maximum and medium security facilities, including Bedford Hills Correctional Facility, Albion Correctional Facility, and Bayview Correctional Facility. The women only experienced minimum security level prisons such as Beacon Correctional Facility prior to being released.

Housing

Of the 17 men, five were residing with their intimate partner and four with their mother. Two of the men were residing in housing available through Fortune Society, and two were homeless at the time of the interview. Two of the men actually had a place of their own. Only one of the men was living with a friend at the time of the interview, and one was living in parole transitional housing.

Many of the men and women did not want to return to their families because they felt that their families were already overburdened, and in many cases their ties with their families were severed as a result of their illegal activity. At the time of the interview, three women were homeless and three women were residing in housing available through the Fortune Society. Two of the women had their own places and two women resided with their mother. One woman resided with a friend. One of the women, who was married, lived with her husband and kids.

Summary

Based on the intake data, the convenience sample selected for this study is representative of the clients the Fortune Society serves. Consistent with the intake data, the majority of participants in this study were men, undereducated, underemployed, unemployed, were parents, and a several were homeless. There are also notable differences between the men and women participants. Women were more likely to have higher educational attainment. For the most recent conviction, women committed more violent offenses than men. Women did not report affiliations with gangs; however, nearly half of the men reported being a member of a gang prior to, during, or after their incarceration. In terms of housing, five of the men were living with their intimate partners whereas only one of the women lived with her husband.

INTRODUCING THE MEN AND WOMEN

The following biographical sketches provide a brief overview of the 29 African American men and women who shared their stories. Their names have been changed to mask their identities. Table 1 and Table 2 also present a biographical overview of the men and women.

The Men

Adam: fifty-three year old. He has three felony convictions. His last conviction was for grand larceny and criminal possession of a forged document. He was sentenced to two to four years. He served two years. He is currently on parole.

Andre: sixty-one year old. He has three felony convictions. His last conviction was for homicide. He was sentenced to 25 to life. He served 23 years in prison and will be on parole indefinitely.

Brooklyn: forty-eight year old. He has two felony convictions. His last conviction was for criminal possession and sale of a controlled substance. He was sentenced to 10 years. He served his entire sentence.

Casper: eighteen year old. His first and only conviction was for second degree robbery. He was sentenced to one to three years and served two years. He is still a gang member and is currently on parole.

Charles: twenty-nine year old. His first and only felony conviction was for motor vehicle theft. He served two and a half years. He was recently charged with domestic violence which was reduced to disorderly conduct for an altercation with his fiancée.

Daveon: twenty-three year old. He has seven felony convictions. His last conviction was for robbery. He was sentenced to and served 13 months. Daveon is currently on probation. He is former gang member.

Henry: twenty-nine year old. He has two felony convictions. His last conviction was for possession of a weapon in the third degree. He served four years.

Jeremy: forty-one year old. He has four felony convictions. His last conviction was for armed robbery. He was sentenced to eight to 16 years. He served 14 years.

Justin: twenty-eight year old. He has three felony convictions. His last conviction was for conspiracy. He was sentenced to three and a half to seven years. He served three and a half years. He is a former gang member.

Kobe: forty-two year old. He has five felony convictions. His last conviction was for robbery. He was sentenced to 10 years and served the entire sentence. He is a former gang member.

Mark: thirty year old. He has two felony convictions. His last conviction was for distribution of a controlled substance. He was sentenced to 10 years in prison and he served nine years. He is a former gang member.

Marshall: twenty-one year old. He has four felony convictions. His last conviction was for armed robbery. He was sentenced to one to three years in prison. He served a year and four months. He is currently on parole.

Nick: forty year old. He has three felony convictions. His last conviction was for conspiracy and sale of a controlled substance. He was sentenced to 10 years. He served eight years and two months in federal prison. He is currently on parole.

Paul: forty-six year old. He has five felony convictions. His last conviction was for sale of a controlled substance. He served six years. He is currently on parole.

Shane: forty-seven year old. He has three felony convictions. His last conviction was for burglary. He was sentenced to 15 years. He served 13 years. He is currently on parole.

Shawn: twenty-eight year old. He has two felony convictions. His last conviction was for robbery. He was sentenced to two to four years and served three and a half years. He is a former gang member and is currently on probation.

Stephon: twenty-four year old. He has three felony convictions. His last conviction was for sale of a controlled substance. He was sentenced to one year in prison. He served nine months. He is a former gang member.

The Women

Ava: thirty-eight year old. Her first and only conviction was for manslaughter and attempted murder. She was sentenced to 10 ½ to 31 years. She served 20 years in prison. She is currently on parole.

Crystal: thirty-three year old. She was convicted of attempted forgery and served two years in prison. She has one prior felony conviction.

Charisma: twenty-four year old. She has three prior felony convictions. Her last conviction was for sale of controlled substances. She was sentenced to a year in prison and served ten months.

Denise: fifty-one year old lesbian. She has three prior felony convictions. Her last conviction was for burglary. She was sentenced to six years to life. She served six years. She is currently on parole.

Kesha:	twenty-four year old. She was convicted of first degree burglary. She was sentenced to and served a year in prison.
Kira:	forty-seven year old lesbian. She has two felony convictions. Her last conviction was for sale of a controlled substance. She served two years in prison.
Mona:	fifty-one year old. Her first and only conviction was for second degree robbery. She served four years in prison. She is currently on parole.
Michelle:	twenty-two year old. She has two felony convictions. Her last conviction was for manslaughter in the first degree. She served two years and six months in prison. She is currently on parole.
Nichole:	forty-four year old. She has three felony convictions, including manslaughter. Her last conviction was for robbery and conspiracy. She served five years in prison. Nichole is currently on parole.
Sara:	thirty-five year old. She was convicted of sale of a controlled substance. She served two years in prison.
Sasha:	twenty- two year old. Her last conviction was for aggravated assault. She was sentenced to a year in prison. She served six months.
Teresa:	twenty-eight year old. Her first and only conviction was for conspiracy. She served two years in federal prison.

Table 1: Biographical Profile of the Men

Participant	*Age*	*Last Conviction*	*Time Served*
Adam	53	Grand larceny	2 years
Andre	61	Homicide	23 years
Brooklyn	48	Criminal possession; sale of a controlled substance	10 years
Casper	18	Second degree robbery	2 years
Charles	29	Motor-vehicular theft	2 ½ years
Daveon	23	Robbery	13 months
Henry	29	Possession of a weapon in third degree	4 years
Justin	28	Conspiracy	3 ½ years
Jeremy	41	Armed robbery	14 years
Kobe	42	Robbery	10 years
Mark	30	Distribution of a controlled substance	10 years
Marshall	21	Armed robbery	15 months
Nick	44	Conspiracy; sale of a controlled substance	10 years
Paul	46	Sale of a controlled substance	6 years
Shane	47	Burglary	13 years
Shawn	28	Robbery	3 ½ years
Stephon	24	Sale of a controlled Substance	9 months

Table 2: Biographical Profile of the Women

Participant	*Age*	*Last Conviction*	*Time Served*
Ava	38	Manslaughter; attempted murder	20 years
Crystal	33	Attempted forgery	2 years
Charisma	24	Sale of a controlled substance	10 months
Denise	51	Burglary	6 years
Kesha	24	First degree burglary	1 year
Kira	47	Sale of a controlled substance	2 years
Mona	51	Second degree robbery	4 years
Michelle	22	Manslaughter	2 ½ years
Nichole	44	Robbery; conspiracy	5 years
Sara	35	Sale of a controlled substance	2 years
Sasha	22	Aggravated assault	6 months
Teresa	28	Conspiracy	2 years

CHAPTER 5

Violence and Reentry: Their Story

CHALLENGES ASSOCIATED WITH REENTRY: MEN

As several men acknowledge, finding employment, stable housing, and resolving parental roles were several challenges they encountered. Consistent with previous literature (Taylor-Greene, Polzer, & Lavin-Loucks, 2006; Petersilia, 2004; Richie, 2001; Rose & Clear, 2001) having a job is the necessary foundation for coping with the other challenges associated with reentry. However, many men return with limited marketable skills and little relevant work experience. The men agree that finding a job is not an easy task. Justin, who recently served three and a half years for conspiracy, observed in this regard: "It's hard to get a job. It ain't easy when you get out." Marshall, who has four felony convictions and recently served a year and four months for armed robbery, acknowledges that "with jobs they would look at my record and tell me I can't work... I can't really get a job, I can go look for a job, but they are going to be like what you got?" Jeremy, who served 14 years for his last conviction of armed robbery, also shares the difficulties associated with actually obtaining a job:

> By just being a felon you have major strikes behind you that's hard for you to get a job, especially my age, I am almost forty years old and I never worked a day in my life. I don't know what it's like to have an honest job, an honest day of work.

Several men acknowledge that race has played a role in limiting their employment opportunities. Justin, who recently served three and half years for conspiracy, states, "Your race is always going to play a part, especially in this society." Similarly Stephon, a former gang member with three felony convictions, remarks:

> If you black and you got a felony and you try to get a job at a store they are going to look at you like you are going to try and rob their store. Plus you got a felony in your background it's definitely going to be hard. You black at that, and I got braids and all that other stuff it takes away from us.

Conversely, Shawn, a former gang member who was convicted of armed robbery, acknowledges that being black means "some doors may never open for you." Paul, who has five felony convictions and recently served six years for armed robbery, echoes Shawn's statement:

> A black man with a conviction is like you are fighting all the time and you can't get out of this cage, you fighting, you fighting, you are fighting but every now and then they will open a door… when they open a door you have to step through that door and do everything you can to stay in that door.

Similarly, Casper, an 18 year old gang member who served two years for second degree robbery, acknowledges that being black:

> Means life is hard, real honesty. It's going to be harder in every aspect. I believe with all honesty I believe if a white person put in a job application somewhere and I put one in and we both have GED's he is going to be picked still. I believe so.

Some of the men were not interested in working right after they were released from prison. Andre, a 61 year old who served 23 years in prison for homicide, expressed why he didn't want to get a job right away.

> I didn't want to work right way. I didn't want to do anything. I wanted to be easy, taste the coffee and just relax and then slowly reintegrate myself back. Coming from a secure environment to freedom out here the cultural shock is

unbelievable. I had to be easy and I had a timeline. The first three months I would like to do this and in six months this and I followed that.

Several men pointed out that their lack of employment made it extremely difficult for them to stay off the streets and avoid the negative peer influence that often accompanies street life. Justin, who recently served three and a half years for conspiracy and Marshall, who has four felonies and recently served a year and four months for armed robbery, described the related challenges of staying off the streets. Justin admits, "Right now I'm still trying to get a job." He said that he has been on a lot of interviews; however, employers continually tell him, "I'm going to call you, I'm going to call you, I'm going to call you. Right now, I'm not trying to hustle." As a result, he acknowledges that, "My support group I don't have one of those. My support group is welfare, food stamps." Justin also admits due to unemployment and lack of funds, "last month I really had to hard [return to crime] to get my daughter some sneakers. I didn't want her [mother of his children] to ask her man for the money so I had to go hard for her." Marshall also admits that, "Staying of the streets" is a challenge. He mentions that when he was first released he informed his mother that he was going to stay out of the streets. Marshall said, "That lasted for about three days, then I was back on the street." Marshall emphasizes that although he was not robbing people, he was around things he was not supposed to be around.

Housing

In terms of housing, as previously outlined at the time of the interview five men were living with their significant other, four were living with their mother, three were homeless, two were living on their own, one was residing in temporary/subsidized housing available through the Fortune Society, one was residing in transitional housing, and one was residing with a friend. Securing housing is a significant challenge. Paul, who has five felony convictions and recently served six years for armed robbery, states:

> When I came home I went to the shelter. I went to Wards Island, the Open Door. The open door is like a walk in emergency, but there are no beds. You have to sleep on chairs… You sleep in chairs, there are no beds. It's like coed. You have men and women there, all over the place.

Adam, who served two years for grand larceny and criminal possession of a forged instrument, states:

> I didn't have any definite place where I was going to be staying at when I got released the second time. I didn't want to stay with my family members because my Mom had already begun taking care of my daughters because of the loss of my significant other, my girlfriend. So what I did I went into a program called Ready, Willing, and Able…I stayed there for a little while. I didn't like the idea of doing the type of work that they had me doing. So I left from out of that program and just started floating around trying to find my way a little bit, trying to find my way.

Brooklyn, who served 10 years for criminal possession and sale of a controlled substance, discussed his dilemma. Due to Brooklyn's prior drug conviction he was unable to live in public housing. As Petersilia (2003) asserts, laws excluding persons with drug felony convictions from public housing make finding safe and stable housing extremely difficult. Brooklyn states, "As far as housing, yes the projects, I was told that I was ineligible because of the drug charges. As a result, Brooklyn has been living in and out of homeless shelters since his release.

Several of the men returned to live with their mothers. Keith, who served 13 years for burglary, has a lot of respect and admiration for his mother. He loves his mother dearly and enjoys the time he shares with her. Keith's mother provided him with his own living space where he is very comfortable. He cheerfully expresses, "it's just me and my moms." He states, "I love my mother to death." Due to his father being absent in his life, his mom served her role as well as the role of his father. As a result, Keith vowed, "I would never be that way with my children." He acknowledges that he and his daughter are, "very, very, close." Keith says he continues to have an excellent relationship with his mother.

Like Keith, after release, Marshall, who has four felony convictions and recently served a year and four months for armed robbery, adores his mother. He states, "I love my mom dukes. She loves me." He was elated to reunite with his mother; he states in this regard that, "I was the happiest person in the world." When Marshall returned home, he engaged in an in-depth conversation with his mother. He vowed to stay off the streets; however, that promise made was short lived.

Justin, a former gang member who served three and a half years for conspiracy, returned to live with his mother. Unlike the relationship Keith and Marshall share with their mother, Justin acknowledges that his relationship with his mother is not that great. Justin observes, "I still have resentment towards her for throwing me in foster care." Justin confesses that the relationship with his mom is rocky and that the stress associated with getting his life back on track has been overwhelming at times. As a result, Justin has violated his parole on three different occasions. Each violation was a result of substance abuse. Justin claims, "I didn't want to hear my mom's mouth." He admits that he would often go out and smoke marijuana before returning home. Afterwards, Justin admits he "was so high," he states "I didn't know what she was talking about. I hear her yelling, that's all I hear."

Similarly, Casper, an 18 year old former gang member who served two years for second degree burglary, expressed considerable resentment towards his mother. Casper, who is one of fourteen kids, was raised by his aunt who he calls his mother. He acknowledged that growing up it was just him and his mother, until she had a child of her own. He explains that things suddenly changed and "anyone could see the difference." Casper and his mother stopped spending time together and his newborn brother was now the center of attention. Casper acknowledged that often times he would ask his mother to buy him clothes. She would say no, but would return home with clothes for his brother.

Although Casper is currently living with his mother, he acknowledged that there is no communication between the two of them. He states, "she comes in from work, she go to do what she got to do and that's it." Casper admits that he just wants his mother to understand what he went through. He states, "I want her to really know that I turned everything around. I'm doing everything so far." Casper recently completed his GED. He exclaims, "I was pushing myself. I didn't know how far I could go until I pushed myself." He is determined to make his mother proud.

Resolving Fatherly Roles

Thirteen of the seventeen men are fathers. Many of the men were quite forthcoming about the relationships with their children, including the sacrifices, obstacles, and often times the selfishness they experienced. They said their children are very important to them and they went to great lengths to try to provide for them. Adam, who served two years for grand larceny and criminal possession of forged instruments, suffered a loss while incarcerated. The mother of his children unexpectedly died from an aneurysm. He states:

> I lost my kids mother while I was incarcerated. That was kind
> of hard because while I was incarcerated, I didn't have any
> idea that she was sick at the time. They [his family] didn't
> want me to know while I was incarcerated that my significant
> other wasn't doing very well.

Adam explained that while preparing for his release, his sister finally wrote him a letter informing him of his girlfriend's illness. Initially, the family thought it was in Adam's best interest for him to serve his sentence without knowing about his girlfriend's condition. He acknowledges, however, "it was devastating to me." Adam strongly believed that they should have informed him earlier of her illness. He confesses that, "it's still difficult to this day to even talk about. It's one of those things that I had to try and overcome."

As a result of his girlfriend's illness and untimely passing, Adam's mother became the primary caregiver of his twin girls. Once released, Adam decided not to become an additional burden on his mother and checked himself into a shelter. He strategically became homeless to ensure that his twin daughters had a place to live. Since his release, Adam acknowledges that he has been, "floating around trying to find my way a little bit, trying to find my way." Despite not having a place a live, Adam realized that his twins' livelihood was more important than his own.

Andre, who served 23-years for homicide, explained that he is rebuilding his relationship with his son. He acknowledges that while serving his 23 year sentence, his ex-wife brought his son to visit him only once. Andre expresses this was a tough visit for him. He states, "she came with her new husband to introduce me to him and wanted me to sign the adoption papers to change my son's name over. Very tough visit for me, but I didn't sign that." Today, Andre recognizes that his life is about family, reintegration, and bonding. He is determined to substantially strengthen the bond with his son.

Nick, who served ten years in federal prison for conspiracy and sale of a controlled substance, openly discusses his love for not only his two children, but his two grandchildren as well. Nick's son is currently in college and his daughter recently took a leave from college after giving birth to her second child. Nick attributes his children's success to his girlfriend and acknowledges that he has "a good woman" and "great kids." Nick, like many of the other men, acknowledges that family is what helps him get through this difficult time. Nick's story, like so many of the other stories, sheds light toward the complexities of the men and women's lives. Even though they encounter many challenges, based on their accounts, they are loving, supportive, and determined to have a better life for themselves and their families.

In addition, Shawn, a former gang member who has several armed robbery convictions, explains the challenges he experienced as a result of trying to juggle spending time with his three children. His children are very important to him and he travels to Staten Island to visit his oldest son, then to Queens to visit his youngest son, and finally another area in Queens to visit his daughter. Shawn is determined to spend time with his children; however, traveling back and forth is an obstacle being that he is currently unemployed. He asserts that the commute is not that bad. However, Shawn states:

> It's just the metro card. When the program [Fortune] gives me the metro I try to use that metro only for the program because if I put another swipe on it, I won't be able to come to the program. So it's kind of difficult, but I have been dealing with

it. My son understands when I can't come and why I can't come.

Mark, a former gang member who served 10 years in federal prison for distribution of narcotics, discussed his family relations. Mark confesses that he is somewhat of "a mama's boy" and he just made some bad decisions in his youth. A father of three boys, Mark is determined to ensure that his sons have a better life than he had. Mark is currently employed and admits that he is "investing in my life for their [his wife and kids] future. He states:

> I am doing most of the support now because my salary is huge. I made it in other words. From being a gang member, from a young adolescent who didn't have all the answers, broken home where I didn't have a father, I am not going to do that to my boys. I am here for them.

Charles, who was recently charged with disorderly conduct for an altercation with his fiancée, discusses some of the challenges he endured with his children. Charles and his fiancée experienced some financial difficulties and, as a result, the family moved into a homeless shelter for a couple of months. Shortly after that, Charles found an apartment for his family to rent. The apartment was severely infested with roaches, however. The infestation was so bad the roaches started "crawling in my daughter's ears and popping up in school in her book bag." Due to the frustration associated with their living conditions and financial crisis, Charles and his fiancée were involved in a domestic dispute. As a result, the entire family was taken to the precinct. Charles states, "they [police] wanted to take somebody to jail, so they took everybody." This was a life-changing experience for Charles. Seeing his children in the jail cell across from him was devastating.

For some men, getting their own life on track was paramount. Jeremy, who served 14 years for armed robbery, explains, "I said to myself I am not going to come home this time worrying about this person and that person. I got to get on track." He acknowledges that it is like "rebuilding all over again." At this point, Jeremy saved a substantial amount of money; however, he came to the conclusion that, "they [his children] were alright for 14 years" and they would be alright until he got his life together. Like Jeremy, Justin, a former gang member who served three and a half years for conspiracy, was focused on getting his own life together. Although the mother of his children constantly calls to arrange for Justin to spend time with his kids, his rebuttal is, "If I was locked up what would you do?" Justin acknowledges, "I have to get myself together." Justin and Jeremy strongly believes that their children would benefit from them taking a little time to rebuild their lives so they could be better providers for their children.

SOURCES OF CONFLICT: MEN AND THEIR PARTNERS

The majority of men openly discussed their intimate relationships and whether the challenges associated with reentry create conflict in their relationships. From their discussions, several themes emerged: 1) efforts to reestablish roles; and 2) issues of infidelity. For the most part, the men provided insight and accounts into the ways in which they believe their intimate partner causes conflict.

Efforts to Reestablish Roles

Several of the men pointed out the difficulties of reestablishing intimate relationships during reentry. Reunited couples face many challenges. Previous literature acknowledges that men's adaptation to prison life impairs their ability to be good husbands, boyfriends, and fathers when they return home (Rose & Clear, 2001). Kobe, a former gang member who recently served ten years for robbery, experienced a lot of difficulties with his girlfriend during reentry. He has been trying to figure out the connection and whether or not the problems experienced in his relationship were related to his prison experience. Kobe served the last four years of his prison sentence in solitary confinement. He states, "I want a relationship, but I want the right relationship. It's bizarre. It's really bizarre. I don't know if prison did that to me, whereas the emotional side of a woman, I can't communicate to women like I should."

Additionally, because prison relieves men of adult roles and responsibilities, it can foster a childlike dependency. Daveon, who has seven felony convictions and recently served three and a half years for conspiracy, when speaking of his situation with his girlfriend states, "she knows right now I can't do as much as I want to do." He acknowledges that as a result of not having a "job a day in my life sometimes we get along, sometimes we don't." Stephon, a former gang member with three felony convictions, expresses similar sentiments; in this regard he reluctantly acknowledges, "my girl she is holding it down now. She is working two jobs. She said as long as I am not going out getting in trouble, and doing what you are not supposed to do, you are fine you can stay here."

Men's efforts to reestablish their role in the relationship created conflict for some of them. Several of the men returned home to existing intimate relationships. In many instances, during the time spent apart, both partners' ideas and expectations about the relationship changed. Several men acknowledge how not being able to provide for the family unit created conflict in their relationships. Justin, a former gang member who served three and half years for conspiracy, experienced conflict with the mother of his child, his ex-girlfriend. He explained how things changed once he was unable to provide when he returned home from prison:

> I don't have any money. She knows I'm not working. She knows it's hard for me to get a job. Her little boyfriend got a little construction job so she looks at me like you ain't shit. You ain't nothing. I look at her like when I was selling drugs and shit I was that nigga to you. I'm focused on my career right now. I'm going hard. I'm treating this finding the job thing like I am selling drugs. I am feigning to get to the top.

Justin further acknowledges the tension between him and his ex-girlfriend. He said she constantly tells him, "You ain't this, you ain't a good father." He argued, "what you mean I'm not a good father? I take my kids to the park. I do everything I have to do with them. I'm a fucked up father because I'm not working?" Consistent with previous research (Oliver, 1989), for some men financial uncertainty may lead to stress that may in turn contribute to intimate partner violence.

Issues of Infidelity

Previous research acknowledges that intimate partner conflict that results in violence is often rooted in men's efforts to control their partner's behavior (Harrison & Oliver, 2006). A number of participants appeared to confirm this dynamic. Although many of the men appear to be controlling in their relationships, they did not acknowledge or own such behavior. Instead they provide justifications for their actions and ultimately blame their female partners. Making accusations of infidelity represents a common way men create conflict with their partners.

The majority of men discussed specifically the ways in which they believe their intimate partners contributed to conflict in the relationship. They did not "own" their behavior, but yet characterized their behavior as being a result of their female partner's inappropriate actions. These narratives are provided in order to give a complete profile of what was understood of the men to be the dynamics of violence. Issues of infidelity were also identified as contributing to conflict in their relationships.

For Kobe, a former gang member who recently served ten years for armed robbery, conflict began in his relationship when differences between him and his girlfriend began to occur. He felt as if he could not be himself around her. He acknowledges that several problems sparked when he wanted to explore different things sexually:

> Sexually it was a lot of things mixed up. I don't know how to tell you this. This is personal. I was away for a long time so I wanted to explore sexually different things and I made her feel uncomfortable with certain things. She made me feel like I couldn't explore. She used to tell me no that make me feel uncomfortable. She was too prissy. She doesn't talk to her friends about sex. I was feeling like she was too fake, but that was the way she was raised, real reserved. I wanted someone different, someone who was sure about their sexuality, willing to explore...a freak. That's what started me probably not paying attention to our relationship and stepping outside of the relationship.

Kobe recalls how things escalated as a result of him stepping out:

> It got crazy. It got to a point where the trust was damaged. I couldn't go anywhere without her where you at? A lot of the times I wasn't doing anything and it was just a real volatile

situation. I started running from that. I don't need that.. I was in prison all of this time. I am self sufficient …I don't need a woman. I don't need to sleep on a woman's couch.

Casper, an 18 year old gang member who served two years for second degree robbery, states:

> We go through stuff. Right now we are going through stuff. We go through a lot. Right now, I be having that feeling like something is not right about it. I trust her, but I be seeing too much stuff. I try to put myself in that position. If I got a girl or if a girl got a boyfriend and I'm trying to talk to her on the low then…on her face book I will see messages she sent but I won't see messages they sent. I know she be deleting it. I can't really say too much about it. I just want to get my stuff right…we are going to just build together.

Casper believes that his girlfriend was cheating on him. He mentions that when they were upset at each other it is usually because she is doing something. He often goes through her cell phone. He describes what it was like:

> I'll look at it and I will give it back to her. She will look at it and she will already know. I wouldn't say nothing. She be like oh it's not what you are thinking. I don't even want to hear it sometimes. I will just leave. I'll be like I see you later.

Marshall, who has four felony convictions and recently served a year and four months for armed robbery, admits that the conflict in his relationships is due to his infidelity. He acknowledges that his girlfriend hears, "stuff from friends that I be cheating and they be seeing me in cars." When asked if he is cheating on his girlfriend, he said, "I ain't going to lie. She heard it like twice. She didn't hear it over a million times. I guess that's enough for her to believe at least something happened." He further states that his mother's neighbor told his girlfriend about him riding with another woman. Ironically, he confessed, "I had sex with her too."

The men discussed various sources of conflict in their intimate relationships. The primary sources of conflict stemmed from their efforts to reestablish their roles in the relationship and dealing with issues of infidelity. In efforts to establish their roles, lack of communication skills, financial dependency, and financial uncertainty contributed to conflict between the men and their intimate partners. Specifically, not having a job and being unable to provide for their intimate partner and children appeared stressful for the men. In regards to infidelity, several of the men committed infidelities; however, they tried to control the behavior of their intimate partners due to their guilty conscious. By their admission, several men were unfaithful to their female partners, yet they wanted to control their partner's behavior.

EXPERIENCES OF IPV DURING REENTRY

Conflict is an inevitable part of intimate relationships. In the absence of proper coping mechanisms or an effective way of dealing with the conflict, violence can ensue (Hairston & Oliver, 2006). Men were perpetrators of emotional and physical violence and also claimed to receive physical and emotional violence from their female partner. For the men, in the majority of the narrative, when first asked about physical violence they responded, "I don't hit females." However, as the interviews went on they revealed something quite different. For the majority of the men, after the admission of resort to physical violence they quickly assumed the role of the victim by asserting that their actions were a reflex or they were simply reacting to their partners' violent behavior.

Emotional Violence

Several men shared their stories about incidents of verbal abuse. Kobe, a former gang member who served ten years for armed robbery, acknowledges that the nature of the fighting between him and his girlfriend was verbal. He explains, "that was the nature of our fighting because it would never go physical. On her part she used to throw stuff, my defense was a verbal lashing." Kobe continues to provide details of his verbal lashing, and admits to calling his girlfriend a "fat, fat bitch, and that was only just to hurt her. It was intentional because I'm not physical… I would like to hurt you because I can't hurt you physically." Kobe explains that the verbal lashing was reciprocal. He acknowledges that his girlfriend would constantly remind him "you will never be nothing." She often referred to him as an "ingrate, jailbird, and a low life." After eight months of verbal abuse, Kobe states, "I was tired. I didn't want to tolerate the stuff anymore." That was the first breakup; however, they go back and forth in their relationship.

Justin, a former gang member who served three and a half years for conspiracy, openly acknowledged the verbal abuse he experienced from his ex-girlfriend and girlfriend. In speaking about his ex-girlfriend Justin observes, "she comes in your face tell you this and tell you that. Just let you feel like you ain't nothing." Justin expressed that because of her behavior he feels, "like I ain't nothing." Paul, who has five felony convictions and recently served six years for armed robbery, acknowledges that arguments were common between him and his girlfriend. He admits they would scream and shout at each other. He describes an incident that occurred one day:

> Yeah she cursed me out one day in the streets... I'm walking we were supposed to be going somewhere. Just come on! It's like I'm her son or something. She talks to me like I am her son. Come on! I left her and got on the train…I paid my fare. I stood there and waited for the train to come. She came in and said, "What you paid your fare for! Get out?! Come on and walked out the door… I said young lady! I tried to catch her. She got out screaming and cursing! She was still walking, she didn't stop…I got on the train and broke out. I am going all the way out to Far Rockaway, that's like a two-hour ride from Manhattan. When I get out there you can't be acting like that. I said I'm out.

Daveon, who has seven felony convictions and recently served three and a half years for conspiracy, said "I'm real respectful. I don't hit females. She will call me names, but I ignore her." When asked about his relationship and whether or not there was any tension or conflict between him and his girlfriend, Brooklyn, who served 10 years for criminal possession and sale of a controlled substance, said, "Of course of course…once again she is very strong-willed and very opinionated. I have learned to separate, that helps me to deal with her more." Casper, an eighteen year old gang member who served two years for second degree robbery, also acknowledges that there is verbal abuse in his relationship. He states they "curse each other out." Physical violence occurs in the relationship as well. He states, "she has hit me but not to hurt me. I will never do that to her, that is not in my nature. Never!"

Physical violence

Six of the men experienced physical violence during reentry. The levels of violence varied greatly. Kobe, a former gang member who served ten years in prison for armed robbery stated in this regard:

> It got physical on her part. She use to throw picture frames and things like that. That is not me. I tend to run from that…when I noticed there was a difference between she and I, when I felt like I couldn't be myself…I'm not saying that I'm not a thug, I am, I really am, that's in me. It probably won't go anywhere; you will see it come out from time to time. I'm not proud of it. I am from the street. I've been to jail all these years. I've been in the streets all these years. I just learned how to be professional.

He continues:

> I wasn't physical, but she would get to physical point throwing stuff. She would do this a lot. She used to run up on me and throw her chest up on me and I'm like what? What? I use to turn her around, push her aside, walk away.

Kobe acknowledges that his girlfriend threw picture frames and an iron at him before. As previously mentioned, several of the men, when asked if they have ever hit a woman, responded, "I don't hit women," however, the next few excerpts provide a deeper insight. Paul explains an incident that he experienced with his girlfriend one day. He expresses that his response to his girlfriend's episodes of violence is "I give her a shake." When trying to make sense of his girlfriend's behavior, he states:

First of all, I know the last person she was with whipped her daily, whipped her crazy. I would never actually put my hands on you, but if she comes at me crazy, I got to. Why you hit me? I am shaking her. I am hitting her. She will tell her family I hit her. They look at her, they know me, and they see me. They will look at her and will be like no he didn't hit her...Nah he didn't hit you.

When asked if he ever hit a woman, Paul responds:

Nah, I don't hit women. I will grab you. I will hold you because she goes crazy. You stop it. I will put you in a bear hug. You can't move. You can't run. "Ahh get off of me. You are abusing me." I am like woman just calm down. I try to calm her down. If you come at me I got to grab you. I got to hold you. I'm not letting you go. So what?

Charles, who was recently charged with disorderly conduct for an altercation with his fiancée, also recalls an incident:

She pushed me, I pushed her. The next thing I know we are wrestling…just pushing and shoving. The neighbor downstairs called the police. The police came and we let them upstairs. We didn't respect them when they came in. They got mad and of course they wanted to take somebody to jail so they took everybody. Me, my kids were in the same jail. I could see my kids hanging their hands out the bars and it was tearing me apart.

When probing further about violence occurring within their relationship, Charles responded:

We are not like that. That one particular day stuff happens. A lot of stuff built up, we didn't talk about it enough the night before, no pillow talk and it got out of the way, that was all it was…I never hit her. I never abused her. She had no marks, I had no marks, it was just pushing and shoving….he called the police to do that.

Marshall provides further insight into the types of violence that sometimes occurs between formerly incarcerated men and their intimate partners. More specifically, he gives us an understanding of how some men perceive their actions as he states:

> She threw stuff at me before and she pulled a knife out too. I told her if she cut me I am going to cut her back. So I guess she thought about it. Over three times I was scuffling with my baby moms... I started saying wild crazy shit. The bitch talking about alright I'm leaving... I said you ain't going nowhere. I started fucking her up a little bit. She was trying but I am a man she's not going to do nothing to me.

While Shawn, a former gang member who served three and a half years for his last conviction of robbery states:

> Yelling and cursing is one thing, but she step in my face, she rolls her eyes, roll her hips and all this other stuff, 'You ain't, shit you ain't never going to be shit, you always going to be a gang member.' That kind of hurts. She punched me like a guy...I was wrong for cheating, okay but you punched me with some strength. So my reaction is to hit back. I can't just take a punch and hold back...She put the flat iron on my shoulder. It burned so bad... I tried to burn her back. It was already unplugged.

And Justin, a former gang member who served three and a half years for conspiracy explains:

> Don't get me wrong, me and my baby mom we fought. She has swinging problems that's one reason why I had to leave her alone... when she don't get her way she will start throwing shit, fight, cussing ...I'm not going to lie, but I hit her back once. She punched the shit out of me. I didn't mean to hit her, but it was kind of like a reflex. My baby mom she hits hard. I had to leave her. I couldn't deal with it.

Summary of Men's Experiences of IPV During Reentry

In summation, there are many challenges that African American men encounter during reentry. Consistent with previous literature, this study found employment and housing challenges for black men. The findings also reveal that reestablishing roles and issues of infidelity are sources of conflict in men's intimate relationships. Furthermore, intimate partner violence occurs in the lives of African American men. Emotional and physical violence were the two primary types of violence experienced by the men in this study. In addition, the men, for the most part, viewed themselves as victims of violence and merely reacting to violence perpetrated by their female partners. They often rationalized their behavior on the grounds that their partners' actions provoked or caused the violence and that they simply reacted to the situation.

In terms of race and gender, the men discussed their experiences as a black man during reentry. The majority acknowledged that race plays an integral part in the opportunities available, especially regarding employment. Andre, who served 23 years for homicide and Charles, who was recently charged with disorderly conduct for an altercation with his fiancé, responses captures the complexities of being a black man during reentry. Andre acknowledges, "being a black man is a proud feeling for me, but it's one that tells me I better be sharp, be careful, and be vigilant being black in American it's not the easiest thing." Similarly, Charles contends, "as black men, we are looked down upon… I think for blacks you always have something to prove." Charles continues, "I am a black man; that doesn't mean that stops me, that just means I have to work harder."

CHALLENGES ASSOCIATED WITH REENTRY: WOMEN

Many of the women's experiences relate to the corresponding literature. Finding employment is a major issue for many women offenders returning to their communities as Richie (2001) has shown. Finding and maintaining a job provides the necessary foundation for coping with other challenges associated with reentry. As the women acknowledge, finding employment and a safe and stable place to live is essential; however, many of the women interviewed returned with few marketable skills and little prior job experience. In general, women's challenges were most commonly associated with gainful employment, safe and affordable housing, mental health services, and resolving parental roles.

Employment

Finding and maintaining a job was a key issue for several women. Mona, who served four years for a crime she was involved in with her husband, observed the following: "I am looking for a job. It's hard. I have a felony and I have robbery in the second degree. It's considered violent." Sasha, who was convicted of aggravated assault against her boyfriend, also acknowledges "it's kind of hard because you have the criminal background that's why I came here [Fortune] so I could get help with that." Similarly, Denise, who has three felony convictions and recently served six years for burglary, noted the following:

> That's what it mostly is for me, employment. The only thing that's helping me now is I'm in a good place at Fortune. It's like none other, no other place. They give you the time, the resources there, they give you the time to sit back and decide what you want to do.

Denise further explains the implications of not having a job:

> This is killing me. I have never been unemployed 6 months in my life. It's been a whole year. Mentally it had the most affect of not having a income. And even public assistance, I can't even get that damn thing. What is it, $80 every 2 weeks? I called yesterday they said $27. I said why? Now I got to go there and find out why. I don't even know why.

Several women discussed the role of race during reentry. Sasha, who was convicted of aggravated assault against her boyfriend, believes strongly that "race plays a part in everything, everything, everything." Ava, who served 20 years for manslaughter and attempted murder, expresses similar sentiments when she states "in America, being black could be really rough, if you are not in certain circles." Charisma, who is currently involved in an ongoing battle with Social Services to regain custody of her son, discusses an illustrative incident that occurred while interviewing for a job:

> When I talk to them on the phone because I can change my voice on the phone, they be like come to the interview, at the interview you can see their face. You know how you can tell they are brushing you off just because you're black? Then I walk back and a white girl got hired… the only time race is a problem is when getting a job.

Although Kesha, who served a year in prison for first degree burglary, found a job, she discusses the difficulties she encountered in maintaining it:

> Well the first job I got I was so excited. I had just came home within like two weeks and it was a maintenance working job. I got the job. They did the background check and they let me go, so I only had that job for a month. Then I had got something off the books through a friend. She was leaving to go to Puerto Rico and was like would you like to take my place in restoration, repairing metal, electricity? Repairing lamps, chandeliers, stuff like that, and I took on to that job for a year and a half, off the books, but it was something.

Housing

Housing was a challenge for some women as well. The majority of the individuals who were homeless and living in temporary housing were women. Ava, who served 20 years for manslaughter and attempted murder, describes in detail her challenges with locating safe and affordable housing. She explains:

> I got out. They came and picked me up and I went to this place called Providence House. I didn't parole to my family. That could be sticky. The family members who agreed with certain things or didn't agree, I didn't want anybody to be like well I am not coming over there because she is there. So I didn't parole to my family. I'm still going through it; housing has been an obstacle for me.

Charisma, whose son was taken by child protective services during a custody battle prior to her last incarceration, describes her housing situation as follows:

> I know it's going to sound weird. I wanted to come home, but when I first came home I didn't want to be home; I really don't have no family. I didn't know where I was going to stay; I am used to being in the streets. I am used to getting fast money. It was kind of like damn, am I going to stay out this time? I kept thinking about my son. I know even now… Get some fast money. I am used to having name brand clothes, hair and nails done up. I am used to having my own apartment, not live in the shelter. It was kind of sad.

Two of the women living in the Fortune Society apartments, however, had different perspectives on their living arrangements. Nichole, who has three felonies including manslaughter, said, "I want out of there [the Fortune Society apartments]. She did not want staff and other residents, "all up in my business." Alternatively, Mona, who served four years for a crime she was involved in with her husband, was grateful and thankful for the services of Fortune Society:

> A lot of people are not that lucky to come out of jail straight to my apartment. They go to a three-quarter house. And I was like wow I can cook food. They gave me emergency food stamps; I hurried up and went and got cold cuts, and soda. I was like somebody that comes from another country. A little kid in a toy store that was me- wow! Somebody pinch me. You just don't know what I have been through. I am alive. I am still like I don't want to wake up.

Kesha, who served a year in prison for first degree burglary, said that finding a place to live has been extremely difficult for her. She has been, "fluctuating from house to house, with friends and family." Kesha states, "I'm a single person with no kids so it's so hard. I can't get into no shelter. I can't get into nowhere. There's no help for nobody single. You have to find a friend, somebody out there to help you."

Mental Health

Several of the women have been diagnosed with mental illness of one type or another and were receiving treatment. Ava, who served 20 years for manslaughter and attempted murder, describes her struggle with mental health issues in the following words:

> They diagnosed me with bipolar manic depression way before I came home from prison. I don't like feed into that. I don't buy into that. First of all, from what I read up on bipolar disorder, not to say I haven't had mood swings or I haven't went through my things with depression, who doesn't go through those things? Who doesn't have ups and downs in their life? I could see you tomorrow and you could say I'm having a bad day. Does that mean you are bipolar because today is a bad day and yesterday was a good day?

Ava explains that going up before the parole board on five different occasions was a bit difficult for her. She continues:

> I took medication at first because I couldn't sleep. I would be up for weeks and that wasn't good. And I said I need to sleep. When I got hit [denied] at the board the fourth time or the fifth time, I went through something. It was like I couldn't get it, I was so like, what are they hitting me for? Why won't they let me go home? I got depressed…I went through something and the doctor was like you need to get some rest. Your body is going to shut down in a minute. I don't want to see that happen. He put me on something that helped me mellow out a little bit. Like somebody had jolted me with a hit of crack.

On the other hand, Mona, who served four years for a crime she was involved in with her husband, her diagnosis came as a result of the crime. Mona explains her diagnosis and assessment of it thusly:

> They diagnosed me with depression and anxiety. That's the diagnosis that they gave me, but that's not really the issue. The issue is I see this man that I love unconditionally kill his girlfriend right in my face. This I have to live for the rest of

my life with this. There is no forgiveness for what this man did. I can never forgive him.

Similarly Nichole, who has three felonies including manslaughter, observed the following:

> I've been diagnosed with psych issues, actually my whole family. I don't know what my mother did to us. I have schizophrenia, bipolar, all of that. I almost got locked up. I went off in the SSI building about my benefits. They called my parole officer. Everything is a challenge to me. Keeping my attitude in check is a challenge.

Although these women have been diagnosed with and treated for mental illness, their challenges do not end there. As Gaes et al. (1999) has shown, in many instances Medicaid has been terminated during their incarceration. Formerly incarcerated individuals have to reapply for Medicaid benefits and go without medication while awaiting the decision on reinstatement of benefits. Mona's sentiments summed things up as she states, "yes I did apply. I am waiting for them to turn me down. They say the first time they turn you down. So all I can do is apply again."

Resolving Motherly Roles

Although eight of the twelve women were mothers, only three women discussed their relationship with their children in any detail. Arguably, as a result of the strained relationships a lot of formerly incarcerated women have with their children, the women did not feel comfortable with discussing this issue. Mona, who served four years for a crime she was involved in with her husband, admits she no longer has a relationship with her grown 35-year old daughter. She explains the situation thusly:

> My daughter turned me in to the police... this is something that I created out of love, carried, and bought into this world. I haven't seen my daughter. She never wrote to me. I lived for two and a half years angry. I don't want to see her because

you see a mother's door is always open, but my doors towards her, they are closed.

Nichole, who has three felony convictions including manslaughter, briefly mentioned her two daughters; however, she did explain that her mother was their primary caregiver while she was in and out of prison. For Charisma, who lost custody of her son prior to going to prison, reunification with her son was her primary concern. She discusses her challenges in this regard in the following words:

> Fighting a custody battle, I have this daughter now, they want to put a case on her but they can't because I've done everything I am supposed to do. I used to do drugs. I have a drug history. I have done some things and when you trying to change and you are trying to put that in your past, your past has a way of creeping out. I am trying to show everybody that I am not the person that I was before, and it's really hard. I didn't lose custody of my son; they took my son for that case which wasn't true. I am fighting a custody battle with my son. My case has been going on for so long they told me to do parenting, they told me to do all these services for them to tell me that they want to give custody back to his father. Now I am just getting pissed.

Similarly, Crystal, who served two years for attempted forgery, discusses some of the issues she experienced with her kids as a result of serving time in prison.

> I am still dealing with the aftermath of my kids with regards to the separation. I have a kid that has ADHD and aggressive disorder; that's what they labeled it as…a lot of it had to do with the fact we were separated and at the time his dad also stopped being in his life. It was an abundance of not only me, watching a lot of the drama unfold while me and his father was together kind of had an effect on him. Now he is in his rebellious stage and he has been a couple times to the hospital. He is ten. I am facing the drawbacks of that right now.

Taken together these accounts illustrate well the types of challenges associated with reestablishing and maintaining a relationship with the children of reentry offenders.   While incarcerated, the women's relationships with their children are strained by limited opportunities for visits due to the substantial distance they are incarcerated away from their homes. In addition, financial hardship and emotional distress suffered by their children as a result of their mother's incarceration have similar adverse effects (see Schirmer, Nellis, & Mauer, 2009; Parke & Clarke-Stewart, 2002; and Richie, 2001). Children of incarcerated mothers often suffer emotionally, financially, and socially and their suffering often times, continues after their mother is released (Schirmer, Nellis, & Mauer, 2009; Murray, Janson, & Farrington, 2007; Parke & Clarke-Stewart, 2002; Richie, 2001). For many incarcerated women, the issues related to the custody of children, repairing relationships, and parenting are stressful. Arguably, as a result of the depth of feeling involved, many of the women refrained from discussing details about their relationships (or lack thereof) due to the emotional challenges that are difficult for them to manage.

EXPERIENCES OF IPV DURING REENTRY

The women experienced intimate partner violence in both physical and emotional ways. Although, the majority of women openly discussed their intimate relationships, they frequently did not pinpoint specific sources of conflict. Two women briefly discussed infidelity as a source of conflict. Nichole, who has three felonies including manslaughter, said that her boyfriend constantly tries to check her phone to see what guys are calling her. As a result, physical violence occurs at times. Similarly, Kesha, who served a year for first degree burglary, admits that the arguments and disagreements between her and her boyfriend were because of suspected infidelity. She states in this regard:

> Jealousy, because I would be the home type. I stayed home, I cooked, I cleaned. I wouldn't go out and party. That just wasn't me. I had siblings that were looking up to me. So I couldn't be out shaking my tail, can't do that. So I would be in the house... He wanted to be out there partying, and I wasn't with it.

Emotional violence

Several of the women experienced emotional violence in their relationships. A few of the women were verbally abused by their intimate partner, and at times the women were verbally abusive. Mona, who served four years for a crime she was involved in with her husband, wants a divorce. Mona's husband is currently incarcerated for the murder of his pregnant mistress, a homicide which Mona witnessed. Mona has been threatened previously by her husband. He told Mona if she leaves him he will kill her. After release from prison and after engaging services through the Fortune Society, Mona's husband contacted her. Mona describes what happened thusly:

> He found me here [Fortune]. I told my counselor the next letter that he sends please send it back. Tell him that I died. Tell him that I no longer come to this program. I am out I don't want no part of you. If you killed this woman you are willing to kill me. I cannot forget that day. Mentally I am messed up. The smell of the blood, the woman gasping…him taking the kitchen knife from ear to ear, I saw the windpipe, saw everything…took the hammer, you know how the head is round? The next thing I know its flat. I am not afraid of him, but I refuse to die from his hands…right now I am living the life hiding from him.

Mona acknowledges that because of the incident that occurred with her husband, she has been diagnosed with a mental illness. She states, "I am taking mental medications right now because this thing that happened. He expects for me to be his wife, to love him. I can't."

A few of the women admit that they are verbally abusing their partners. Nichole, who has three felonies including manslaughter, admits, "I argue and he just has to accept that." Crystal, one of the few women who were married, discusses her relationship with her husband. As she states, "I think our outlooks are different, because I was pretty much raised in the streets I think I am a little more abrupt than he is." When asked if there has there been any cursing or yelling in the relationship, Crystal responds as follows:

> Yes and I know the ideology is that its verbal abuse and I know the stigma that comes along with that. At the same time, I think I can tolerate that more so than what I was going through with my ex. He was physically abusive. He temporarily paralyzed me. He snapped my back because I didn't want to be with him anymore. He said if I can't have you can't nobody else have you.

Crystal also acknowledges that one incident of physical violence occurred in which she initiated the violence, explaining, "yeah, yeah, yeah. I think that comes from me being abused and the whole ideology that this is how you deal with conflict. He was ready to leave. I had to kiss and make up and play nice."

<u>Same-sex violence</u>

As previously outlined, three of the women identified themselves as lesbians and were currently involved in same-sex relationships. They provided intricate details about the types of violence that occurred in their intimate relationship. Denise, who has three felony convictions and served six years for burglary, characterizes the issues she experienced with the woman she has been dating for seven months thusly:

> Well it's fine. Well to be honest it's Ok. I want to go a little slower. I love her, I'm not really in love with her, but I love her. Its tension sometimes, cause I have to make an account for every tiny thing. I'm not used to that. That reminds me of controlling, makes me think that you're trying to be controlling. First of all I'm too dominant for that. I don't mind compromising, but I know what abuse looks like and it makes me think controlling. It has to be a certain amount of trust here. She's used to being in control, people answering so that's where we clash at. We had two arguments in seven months just cursing and yelling.

Upon reflection, Denise acknowledged that recently her girlfriend initiated an argument after Denise became ill and did not feel well enough to visit her. Denise stated that instead of her girlfriend just understanding that she did not feel good, she assumed that Denise was possibly out cheating. Denise affirmed, "it's nothing else behind it. Why should it be? I told her I've never given you a reason to think anything other so I don't want to hear that kind of stuff."

For Teresa, who served two years in federal prison for conspiracy, her experiences were related to her controlling behavior and personality. Teresa admits, "I have an attitude. That's just who I am. I am real bossy." When asked how her girlfriend deals with her being so controlling, Teresa claims, "she likes it because she is submissive." However, Teresa freely admits that the extent of her submissiveness is "aggravating" at times. As a result of Teresa trying to control her girlfriend, she acknowledges that her partner often reminds her that "I am not out to get you. I am your friend; I am not your enemy." In response to her controlling behavior, Teresa remarks, "it's just in me. I have to get over that."

Kira, who has two felony convictions and served two years for her last conviction of sale of a controlled substance, discusses the different levels of violence experienced in the various relationships she had with several women:

> You know some of them I was in just basically… I was using them to get where I needed to go. Then it became abusive and we were fighting. I wasn't stable you know. Mentally, emotionally, physically, spiritually I was bankrupt all across the board and I was trying to have a relationship or love somebody then I wasn't loving myself. I felt like they were obligated to do certain things for me because of what I did for you. They was creeping and cheating, so it became one lie after another… then next thing you know it became verbal and then physical.

Continuing, Kira states, "I was in an abusive relationship. I don't know that's kind of touchy…You not doing what you supposed to do so now we arguing and fighting because of that." As these accounts illustrate, many of the women experienced emotional violence in their relationships. At times they were on the receiving end of verbal abuse, at other times they verbally abused their intimate partners. Regardless of whether the women were involved in heterosexual or same-sex relationships, intimate partner violence occurred.

Physical violence

Several of the women who experienced physical violence in their relationships shared their stories. Charisma, who is currently involved in a custody battle with Social Services to regain custody of her son, started a relationship with one formerly incarcerated man who received reentry services through the Fortune Society. She explains how the problems with their relationship began:

> He was going with this girl. Around August he broke up with her... the end of my pregnancy the girl pops back up. Not only did she pop back up, she comes and tries to fight me while I was pregnant. I am trying to kill the bitch! It got so bad I even tried to beat up my baby father... nerve damage in my finger because we fought... You see my hands? He bit my finger. You see my bald spots? We have had physical altercations over this, over her. It's being really ridiculous. We had a fight in front of his mother. He dragged me out of his mother's house; we had a fight over the girl. When I was pregnant he used to pin me down, bruise my face."

When asked if she fought him back she states, "of course I fought him back! You should see his god damn face!" After recalling this incident Charisma acknowledges:

> Abuse is not acceptable at all. Sometimes I don't feel like I am pretty enough. Sometimes I have low self-esteem. I just have to tell myself I'm not ugly. It's not me. It's just we weren't meant to be...I need to stop thinking about men and think about myself, love myself truly first.

In several of the relationships described, the women were perpetrators of violence. Nichole, who has three felonies including manslaughter, said, "I have a lot of violent crimes and a lot of violent issues. I have been in a lot of violent relationships. Sometimes, you know how they say, the woman is always the victim? But that is not the case here. I hit on my man or my girl." Nichole admits that she would throw things at him. She also confesses, "I bit him in his forehead. He is wearing that mark." Nichole expresses that she knows "it's really not good." She admits that she verbally abused him as well, and states in this regard, "he doesn't curse I do. I am like fuck you! He's like what? Can you stop cursing? I'm like don't tell me what to do in my house!" Nichole describes an incident with her boyfriend:

> So I open the door. He is looking all deranged in the face. The nigga tried to push his way in the doorway. We tussling…I lose my balance…Why I got to tussle with you for my shit [cell phone]? Before I knew it that nigga was like, slap, slap, slap…in my head. I was like let me get this knife and start poking his ass… I told him about it later on.

Similarly, when asked if there was ever any physical violence in her relationship Kesha, who served a year for first degree burglary, remarked, "of course it was. I was the abusive one, which would be so surprising." She admits that she abused him and that she would, "lock him out, if he didn't get my things" and also throw "tantrums" and start "throwing things at him." She started, "kicking and biting and punching and pulling," while he would just sit there. She states, "he wouldn't harm me for nothing in the world." But, "one day he got fed up and he pushed me. That's the only thing he ever did was just push."

Likewise, Sasha, who was convicted of aggravated assault against her boyfriend, states, "we would often fight. I am not the type of woman that would let a man or anyone else just put their hands on me and act like I can't defend myself… he would verbally and physically abuse me as well." Sasha's comments offered insight into how many of the women viewed strength in their experiences with intimate partner violence. The women equated strength with the ability to endure, fight back, and survive an abusive relationship. This resiliency aided in raising the women's ability to empower themselves to be active in dealing with violence (Potter, 2008).

The majority of women were insistent about protecting themselves and not allowing their intimate partners to hurt them without defending themselves. Kesha, who served a year for first degree burglary, observed that, "it is hard, but yeah I still find myself having the tendencies to put my hands on someone, if I don't get my way." Kesha expresses the sentiments of the majority of women in this study when she notes:

> The first guy that ever put his hands on me that was just for me running my mouth, and he was upset, and I think I said something about his mother and not knowing that she had passed on…He hit me real hard, and I had a big eye jammie for like 14 days. That's what happened and ever since then it was just like, I'm not going to be no one's victim.

The women's stories about their experiences with intimate partner violence are compelling. To fully explore what is happening in their lives, one must move beyond the powerful storylines toward an analysis indicative of their stories on a much deeper level. When asked, what it meant to be a black woman, an overwhelming majority acknowledged that it meant "strength." Charisma proclaims, "black is beautiful, it's strong, and it means struggle. Similarly, the women viewed themselves as "a strong black woman."

Before incarceration, the majority of women had a history of abuse at the hands of their intimate partners; however, they survived, and as a result they refused to become a victim again. As such, there was a significant rejection of the victim label. This rejection was a source of agency and power for the women. Many of their experiences relate to the corresponding literature; rejection of the victim label is common for African American women as Potter (2008) has shown. She asserts that black women are less inclined to label themselves as victims and more inclined to fight back than white women. Fighting back gives them a sense of agency and provides a source of power for women within their intimate relationships. As Hillary Potter (2008) argues, the portrayal of black women as strong, independent, and resilient- clearly positive qualities- has the potential to characterize black women in ways that allows us to understand why they tend to restrict them from seeking help or needed support. This trait often helps African American women to verbally and physically retaliate against their abusers.

Summary of Women's Experiences During Reentry

In summation, the women interviewed for this study encountered many challenges during their reentry experience. As previous research has shown, finding steady gainful employment, securing safe and affordable housing, dealing with mental health issues, and resolving mothering roles were common challenges for these women. These findings also revealed that infidelity is frequently a source of conflict in women's intimate relationships. Intimate partner violence occurred often in the lives of African American women, with emotional and physical violence being the two primary types of violence experienced by these women. Women were both victims and perpetrators of emotional and physical violence. In several of the cases where physical violence occurred, the women were the perpetrators; when violence was perpetrated upon them by their male partners, the women did not act as passive victims, but rather they fought back with vigor.

In terms of race and gender, the women discussed the challenges of being a black woman experiencing reentry. The majority of women acknowledged that race plays an integral part in the opportunities available, especially in regards to securing employment. They also discussed what it means to be a black woman reentering society. Sasha, who was convicted of aggravated assault against her boyfriend, acknowledged the criminal justice system not only captures black men but, "they also have ways of getting us caught up, I mean us black women." Crystal, who served two years for attempted forgery, states in this regard, "for me, being a black woman with a felony has this stigma." Similarly, Denise, who has three felony convictions and recently served six years for burglary, expresses the belief that, "being a black woman, it's a lot less opportunities." Mona acknowledges, "we get discriminated on, but that's been going on for years and that's going to stay here. Kira's statement below captures the essence of what the women were describing. She states:

> Even though I know that there are differences, I just live my life...I see it, but I don't see it. I'm African American that's how I classify myself. I'm proud. I enjoy being African American. I enjoy being a woman. I do. It just means to me like right now where I am in my life, it means that I have to work harder. I feel like I need to take my place in my life and

as well as in society…I'm doing what I need to do, but I'm so far behind.

COMPARATIVE ANALYSIS

Men and women shared common issues related to reentry. Securing employment and obtaining housing is a challenge for many formerly incarcerated men and women. Men and women both have problems with finding and maintaining a job. Although housing is a challenge for both men and women, several gender differences for housing are identified. Women were more likely to report living in homeless shelters or temporary housing than men. The women were reluctant to return to live with family members because of severed ties. Men were significantly more likely to report living with their mothers or significant others than women. The men with children talked extensively about their relationships and the obstacles and challenges that they endured. The men provided detailed information about their children including their ages, achievements, and accomplishments.

The majority of women, to the contrary, were not as forthcoming. This indifference could possibly be attributed to the roles mothers and fathers serve in the lives of their children. Often women were the primary caregivers of their children prior to incarceration, and their relationship with their children became strained as a result of their criminal behavior. As well, women experienced unique challenges associated with mental health issues which the men did not identify as a challenge. Consistent with previous studies, women prisoners in our sample have a higher rate of mental health problems than do men. At midyear 2005, roughly three-quarters (73%) of all women in state prison had mental health problems, compared to 55% of men (James & Glaze, 2006).

Sources of Conflict

When dealing with sources of conflict in intimate relationships, infidelity was a primary issue for men. The women refrained from providing sources of conflict, with the exception of two women who acknowledged infidelity as a source. It was common for men, and not for women, to try and reestablish roles in their intimate relationships since the majority of men returned home to an existing relationship.

Reestablishing the role as primary provider, however, created conflict in many of their relationships due to the fact that men were no longer the breadwinner.

Experiences of IPV During Reentry

Intimate partner violence is a serious issue in the lives of formerly incarcerated men and women during reentry. Physical and emotional violence remain the two primary types of violence that men and women experience during the reentry process. Reciprocal violence occurred in lives of many men and women during this process. Men were both perpetrators of physical violence towards intimate partners with, in most instances the mother of their children, as well as victims of emotional and physical violence. When speaking on violence against their intimate partners, the majority of men viewed themselves as the victim. They often spoke in terms of defending themselves against their female partners. In comparison, men were more likely to be involved in physically violent relationships than were women. This finding could possibly be due to the fact that men more often than women returned to existing relationships. In many cases the women with whom they were involved prior to entering prison were still around when they returned from prison.

Regardless of the type of relationship, heterosexual or same-sex, women seemingly were more likely to be involved in a relatively new relationship with less physical violence, but featuring more emotional violence. When physical violence occurred in the relationship, however, the women were actually perpetrators of violence. The majority of the emotional violence that occurred in their relationships was perpetrated by the women, as well. The women who engaged in violence admitted to and accepted responsibility for their actions; however, the men, for the most part, viewed themselves as victims and merely responding to violence perpetrated by their female partners.

Summary

Formerly incarcerated African American men and women move within a racially charged symbolic universe that effects how they come to understand themselves and are understood by others. As objects of public policy, they are treated severely in part because of their association with an oppressed group in a historical in social context of racial hierarchy (Martin, 2013). Despite the trials and tribulations the black men and women endured during reentry, one common theme present throughout their stories is that of undying hope. Regardless of their varied personal experiences, they remain optimistic. Many experienced discrimination and faced inequities based on race, gender, and class, but nonetheless did not lose hope. They continue to better themselves by taking advantage of the numerous programs and services offered by the Fortune Society. Although many were mandated to participate in certain programs, others willingly sought services at the Fortune Society. Andre, who served 23 years for homicide, is determined to succeed. With a bachelor's degree, Andre sketched out a detailed timeline for achieving certain goals. He began by volunteering as a teacher at the Fortune Society. After three months, Andre was hired. Andre is living his dream, now lecturing at a community college in New York City. Despite multiple hardships, Andre pressed forward and is now fulfilling his dream.

Many of the men and women, like Andre, were able to walk away with something quite positive from their prison experience. He states in this regard:

> The prison experience was very rough for me. I hated to say so in the beginning, but I have come to learn that was absolutely necessary for me…Prison for me was right and exact at that time. That's where I needed to be at that time and my prison experience was a mind-blowing, mind-awakening experience for me, and I am grateful even for that. I was able to survive that and come out of that a physical and mental giant.

Shawn, a former gang member who was convicted of armed robbery, was able to turn his near-death prison experience into something positive as well. While in solitary confinement, Shawn tried to commit suicide. He related the following account of that experience:

> I tried to give up. I put a rope around my neck…when I went for the rope I looked at myself in the mirror and I was so embarrassed. If I hadn't seen myself in the mirror who knows what would have happened…just looking at myself I felt disgusted. I embarrassed me.

Shawn expresses the idea duty to others which came to him while contemplating suicide; in this case he started thinking of his son. He posed the question, "what am I going to tell me son?" He decided, "I can live with this." Shawn put down the rope down, calmed himself down, and got through that difficult time in his life. Recently, Shawn's son told him that he wants to be like him when he grows up. He states:

> That was the best thing I have heard since I have been home. Be like me? I was thinking I should tell him don't say that. He believes his daddy is great. Through the trials and tribulations he believes in me. I am trying to keep my tears to myself, but my son loves me to death. That's my motivation right there. That's my superhero.

In retrospect, Shawn emphasizes the point that his prison experience allowed him to recognize the people "who believes in me, even when I am wrong." Most importantly, Shawn states, "I felt loved, I felt appreciated, after all these years, after all of my wrongdoings, I felt good about myself. I felt good about my situation."

Men who have faced the toughest of times, adversities, and at times near death experiences, express the optimistic view that there is still hope for a better future. Jeremy, who served 14 years for armed robbery, had never worked a legitimate job, and despite the many obstacles in his pathway to the future, is now gainfully employed. Men like Nick, who served ten years in federal prison for conspiracy and sale of narcotics, and Daveon, who has seven felony convictions, like Jeremy had never worked a legitimate job, but nonetheless remain hopeful. Despite employers who constantly tell them they will call and never call, they persistently submit job applications, faithfully participate in career development programs, and remain optimistic in the face of adversity. Barry, who served ten years for sale of a controlled substance, captured the sentiments of many of the men when he stated:

> Regardless of my ups and downs, my trials and tribulations, I have grown to a point that I have become more responsible to myself and for myself. Regardless of whatever is out there that stand against us [blacks] I still posses the ability, the capability, and the determination to knock those stigmatisms down.

Keith, who served thirteen years for burglary, is determined to open a unisex salon and a beauty supply store. Although he has faced many obstacles, Keith states, "I have a bank account, a savings account, a visa card, a debit card. I'm alright. It's slow, but I got plans. I am going to make it happen." This determination is present throughout the men's stories. They have faced adversity and struggled along the way, yet they are still determined to prevail.

The women also expressed determination and hope. Charisma, who is currently involved in a custody battle with Social Services to regain custody of her son, is determined to succeed despite her noteworthy obstacles. She observes in this regard:

> I sat in that program [career development] and I was pregnant. I worked in another job training program, pregnant. Working maintenance and I went to the GED program in here. I did every single group there was upstairs in family services, pregnant…I have potential. I am trying to do something with myself and I think that is the biggest thing. Right now I am struggling, but at least I am making an effort.

Likewise, Kira- who was the valedictorian of her class and received a scholarship to become a certified public accountant- admits "I messed it all up and I regret it." Kira is also determined to better herself and make something positive of her life. She currently works at Riker's Island and she prays every day that with the grace of God she will have enough time to get her life together.

The men and women cannot be defined simply by their problems. Their lives are highly complex, entirely unique, and fascinating- particularly given their need to struggle against iniquitous odds. They tend to take joy in life, with hopes of a better tomorrow. The men and women alike remain optimistic and believe that their futures are promising. No matter the circumstances, as Mona, who served four years for a crime she was involved in with her husband, candidly states, "you cannot break my spirit." Their spirits remain intact, and arguably cannot be broken.

CHAPTER 6

Reflections

Using a blended methodology that included an intersectional and comparative analytical framework, this study explores the ways in which race, gender, and class intersect to structure experiences of intimate partner violence among African American men and women during reentry after prison incarceration. While many researchers have directed their efforts toward employment, housing, healthcare, and family reunification, little attention has been directed toward African American men's and women's experiences of intimate partner violence during reentry. This study attempts to enhance the existing sparse literature in this area; to this end, four main questions are addressed in this study. These questions are: (1) What are the socioeconomic experiences of African American men and women during the reentry process? (2) How are their experiences similar and different? (3) What role does intimate partner violence play during the reentry process? (4) How are African American men and women's experiences similar and different in this regard? A discussion of the findings is presented below, including implications for theory development, reentry practices, and public policy. Implications for future research are sketched in a conclusion to this final chapter.

FINDINGS

Staff interviews reveal several important findings worthy of reiteration here. Formerly incarcerated African American men and women face numerous challenges when reentering society, among them being finding and maintaining gainful employment, securing safe and affordable housing, and negotiating relationships representing the most pressing and pertinent issues. The findings reported here also reveal that intimate partner violence occurs frequently in the lives of formerly incarcerated African American men and women, and these often shape their reentry experiences in several ways. During reentry, intimate partner violence often plays a part in individual court proceedings regarding visitation privileges and orders of protection. On another level, intimate partner violence influences the level of commitment that formerly incarcerated men and women may have in regards to reentry programming relating to job training, employment services, and anger management classes. In essence, intimate partner violence frequently exacerbates the difficulties and challenges faced by many African American men and women. These findings provide insight into the complex nature of IPV and how men and women experience such violence. The findings reported here also show how race plays a role in men's and women's experiences of intimate partner violence and differences between the men and women offenders.

The findings reported here suggest that violence experienced by formerly incarcerated men is likely a consequence of their inability to resolve conflicts effectively. Moreover, the findings documented in this study also reveal that social class shapes experiences of IPV, whereby in the absence of resources formerly incarcerated individuals have to deal with their complex feelings and often intense emotions based on the limited coping mechanisms and skills they already possess developed in institutional correctional settings. Oftentimes, the ways in which many formerly incarcerated men and women deal with these emotions is not the most effective way for the world outside of prison walls.

In terms of addressing the needs of these men and women experiencing reentry, the findings reported here suggest the presence of several organizational barriers- most importantly, the lack of IPV programs and under-trained correctional and post-release transition staff. Intimate partner violence is clearly a commonly experienced problem during reentry; however, neither correctional staff nor those staff associated with organizations such as the Fortune Society were adequately trained to address this issue. Although Fortune Society staff agreed a more substantial role could be undertaken to address intimate partner violence, IPV was not viewed as a priority concern within the organization. For example, staff members repeatedly cited referrals to other agencies and use of an admittedly ineffective anger management program to address men's issues of violence as frequent steps taken to dealing with intimate partner violence that occurs in the lives of formerly incarcerated men. Given the nature of the Fortune Society and their mission, part of the findings reported here can be generalized to other communities as the challenges that many formerly incarcerated individuals encounter are likely quite similar throughout the country.

Formerly Incarcerated Clients

This study reveals that both men and women share many common issues related to reentry after serving time in prison. Securing gainful employment and obtaining safe and affordable housing is a challenge for many formerly incarcerated men and women alike. Many have problems finding employment at all and maintaining a job once secured is a second challenge for many. Although housing is a common challenge for men and women alike, several gender differences with respect to housing were identified. Women were more likely to report living in homeless shelters or temporary housing than were their male counterparts. The women were reluctant to return to live with family members because of severed ties. Men were significantly more likely to report living with their mothers or significant others than were women. Men with children often talked extensively about their troubled relationships and the challenges they endured. They provided detailed information about their children, including their ages, achievements in school, and accomplishments in life. Contrarily, the majority of women were not nearly as forthcoming in this regard. This apparent indifference could possibly be attributed to the roles mothers and fathers serve in the lives of their children. Oftentimes women are the primary caregiver of their children prior to incarceration, and their relationship with their children becomes strained as a result of their criminal behavior. In addition, more women than men experienced challenges associated with mental health issues further complicating the rebuilding of family ties.

When dealing with sources of conflict in intimate relationships, infidelity was a primary issue for men. The women generally refrained from providing infidelity-based sources of conflict, with the exception of two women who acknowledged freely that infidelity was a source of conflict for them. The majority of men returned home to an existing relationship; this was not the norm for female counterparts. Difficulties encountered in reestablishing the role as primary provider, however, created conflict in many of the men's relationships; most were no longer able to assume the "breadwinner" role in the reunited family unit.

Intimate partner violence occurs frequently in the lives of formerly incarcerated African American men and women during reentry, and it is usually characterized by a reciprocal pattern of abuse. Emotional and physical violence remain the two primary types of IPV that men and women of this study experienced. Men claimed to be both perpetrators of physical violence and victims of emotional and physical violence, in most instances with the mother of their children. When physical violence occurred the men, for the most part, viewed themselves as victims. They offered statements that blamed their female partners and explained that their actions were in defense of their livelihood. Furthermore, they argued that they were simply reacting to violence perpetrated by their female partners. In doing so, the men explained that the behavior they exhibited was a reaction to the behavior displayed by their female partners, or that they were only responding to the violence initiated by her. In comparison, men were more likely to be involved in physically violent relationships than the women. This finding could possibly be due to the fact that men returned to pre-existing relationships; the women with whom they were involved prior to entering prison were still around when they returned from prison.

Regardless of the type of relationship with regard to heterosexual or same-sex couples, the women seemingly were more likely to be involved in a relatively new relationship with less physical violence, but experiencing more emotional violence. At the occurrence of physical violence in the relationship, the women fought back. Consistent with previous literature, African American women are more likely to fight back than white women (Potter, 2008). At times, a few women were actually perpetrators of such violence, and the majority of the verbal abuse that occurred in their intimate relationships was perpetrated by the women. Unlike the men, women who were perpetrators of violence admitted to it and accepted responsibility for their actions.

THEORECTICAL AND PRACTICAL IMPLICATIONS

Crime control is a shared responsibility of the individual, the community, and the state and it is most effectively achieved through prevention efforts (Pranis, 1993). Drawing from the study's findings, a restorative justice based prevention program is necessary to help formerly incarcerated African American men and women prevent intimate partner violence. Specifically, intimate partner violence prevention programs based on restorative justice principles are needed to help facilitate the successful reintegration of African American men and women incarcerated offenders into the community. In this study, the majority of men and women experienced IPV during reentry, yet specific IPV programs are neither broadly offered nor readily accessible for those in need. Given the lack of attention to IPV during reentry, it should be expected that men and women returning from prison will continue to have unresolved issues related to violence and intimate partner abuse. It follows that providing an effective intimate partner violence prevention program is a critical necessity at this time in a nation wherein the mass incarceration phenomenon has produced a flood of reentry populations into our local communities.

The findings reported in this study strongly suggest that formerly incarcerated African American men and women require targeted assistance in reuniting with their intimate partners or when establishing new intimate relationships, in order to avoid engaging in behavior that may lead to intimate partner violence or probation or parole revocation. For example, men who experience change in their role as the provider, due to their incarceration and subsequent unemployment, require assistance in managing their feelings and behavior toward women with whom they formerly maintained an intimate relationship and/or is the mother of their children. Women also require assistance in dealing with past hurts and experiences of intimate partner violence, whereby they will be less likely to resort to violence as a means of coping with unresolved issues. Restorative justice based intimate partner violence prevention programs will assist and challenge men and women to accept responsibility for their past actions, restore their dignity and self respect, and empower them with the necessary skills to start rebuilding their lives.

Intimate partner violence prevention programs based on principles of restorative justice should be created to assist formerly incarcerated African American men and women with dealing with potential conflict within their intimate relationships. In many cases, intimate relationships have been broken as a result of the formerly incarcerated individuals' criminal behavior. Often times, these relationships need to be repaired and restoring relationships is the essence of restorative justice. By utilizing a restorative justice framework, such programs could be a valuable contribution to the lives of the formerly incarcerated individuals, their intimate partners, and the communities to which they return upon release. A restorative justice based IPV prevention program should incorporate several key elements: (1) restore the offender's dignity and self respect; (2) promote healthy intimate relationships; (3) provide culturally competent, culturally-specific, and gender-specific staff training pertaining to IPV; (4) employ behavioral, emotional, and cognitive strategies; and (5) empower formerly incarcerated individuals with the necessary skills to start rebuilding their lives.

Such programs should seek to provide assistance for formerly incarcerated offenders in order to avoid further offenses, specifically IPV. To achieve these challenging goals, reentry service providers should assume a proactive role in developing extensive staff trainings, IPV and reentry curricula, and programs that address the intersection of race, gender, and class and intimate partner relationships as a component of comprehensive prisoner reentry initiatives designed to reduce prisoner recidivism and victimization. Restorative justice IPV prevention programs must be culturally competent, culturally sensitive, and gender responsive to address the needs of the many African American men and women coming out of the incarceration over the course of the next decade. Critical race theory contends that the perspectives of the oppressed group must be better understood by the larger society. As previously outlined, several staff referred to violence as normal for formerly incarcerated African American men and women. It should be noted that intimate partner violence is not acceptable and it is not a normal event within African American communities. The fact that staff members viewed the violence in African American men and women's relationships as being a normal part of the relationship provides another barrier to addressing the needs of these men and women. If staff members consider intimate partner violence as an accepted norm within African American communities, it may be perceived as common, expected, and undeserving of much attention. In order to adequately address the issues of IPV, specifically for African Americans, staff members must be trained and educated about cultural and gender differences and how these factors can affect reentry, and ultimately, intimate partner violence. Staff members should receive training that values diversity and have cultural knowledge of the individuals and communities they serve, providing an environment where African American men and women will feel comfortable discussing issues in relation to IPV. In doing so, staff members will be able to assess their own values, attitudes, and beliefs about African Americans as well as recognizing and addressing individual biases and identifying areas for growth. With diversity and cultural training, staff members will be better equipped to recognize the cultural explanation for behaviors such as black women resisting care from formal service providers.

Due to the experiences of formerly incarcerated African American men and women, such programs must also be gender responsive and address the influence of the social constructions of masculinity and femininity in intimate partner violence. For example, in the absence of traditional markers of masculinity, educational achievement, financial and occupation stability, African American men have embraced unconventional expressions of masculinity that often involve the use of violence against their female partners as a means of gaining control and power (Hampton, Oliver, & Magarin, 2003). In other words, some men abuse their female partners as a way of imposing authority and exerting control. Violence, therefore, represents an attempt by men to exercise some form of power and control over women's lives, to assert their will over women's lives in ways that could result in harm, injury, and even death (Garfield, 2005). For formerly incarcerated African American women who "fight back" with their male partners, it is important to understand why they are fighting back and provide skills that will allow them to assert agency in a more constructive way within their intimate relationships. Therefore, it is crucial that IPV prevention programs are gender-specific to address the issues that men and women encounter as a result of belonging to a particular group. Critical race feminism helped to explain the importance of gender during the reentry process. Much of the current literature over generalizes the experiences of men, reflecting the relative invisibility of women in American society. It is necessary that IPV prevention programs place African American women at the center rather than at the margin of such programs, focusing on the gendered and racialized aspects of IPV with hopes of developing appropriate solutions for African American women.

Intimate partner violence is generally a very complex issue, and staff members explained that many formerly incarcerated African

American men and women are ill-equipped to deal effectively with their frustration, fear, and aggressions. These are crucial observations that should be addressed during reentry. It is imperative that intimate partner violence programs teach participants various ways to eliminate stress, as well as increase their ability to cope with stress in appropriate ways. Such programs should employ behavioral, emotional, and cognitive strategies to assist men and women with coping with stress, anger, and anxiety. When they learn alternative strategies to handle conflict in their intimate relationships, then they possibly will be less likely to resort to violence when they encounter stress and conflict within their intimate relationships.

Given the findings reported in this study a restorative justice intimate partner violence prevention program that equips formerly incarcerated men and women with necessary skills and strategies provided by trained professionals is essential to an effective reentry effort. Strengthening relationships between formerly incarcerated men, women, and their intimate partners will require identifying potential sources of conflict in their relationships. Formerly incarcerated individuals must be able to own their behavior and understand how it can possibly affect others. Restorative justice IPV prevention programs will provide an atmosphere within which men and women can express their feelings, tell their stories, and in the process develop problem-solving and conflict- resolution skills that will provide them with alternative strategies to address conflict in their relationships. Implementing an intimate partner violence prevention program with restorative justice principles will allow formerly incarcerated offenders to take responsibility for their past, current, and future actions.

The researcher acknowledges that incorporating the community into a restorative justice based IPV prevention program could present numerous problems. Therefore, given the limitations of larger structural issues and structural constraints, a restorative justice based prevention initiative should be programmatic-specific instead of community-specific. There are several potential benefits associated with implementing IPV prevention programs of such nature during reentry. One potential benefit is a forum where formerly incarcerated African American men and women can talk these critical areas through. The availability of such intimate partner violence prevention programs is essential to ensure that formerly incarcerated men and women's efforts to become contributing law-abiding members of society are not undermined by the lack of skills and tactics needed to deal with issues that could possibly lead to intimate partner violence. Participation in the prevention program can ultimately provide African American men and women with a sense of empowerment and a sense of control of one's life as they make the transition back into their respective communities. Secondly, IPV prevention programs will increase our understanding of sources of conflict for formerly incarcerated men and women who return home to their communities. In doing so, it will increase community awareness of these issues that may in turn decrease crime incidence rates.

CONTRIBUTION TO THE LITERATURE

This study contributes to the literature in a number of ways. First, this work represents one of the few studies that provided an opportunity for African American men and women to discuss in great detail their interpretation of their experiences with intimate partner violence during reentry. In doing so, this study adds to our body of knowledge of reentry by offering their unique experiences, perspectives, and addressing the limitations of past studies that confine analysis of prisoner reentry and intimate partner violence to men with limited attention to women. Secondly, by exploring the role that race, gender, and class play in shaping the experiences of formerly incarcerated men and women, this work highlights the complex nature of IPV and facilitates a deeper understanding of what may be happening to men and women returning to their communities from prison. In doing so, the focus on how race, gender, and class frame the experiences of these men and women creates new questions for investigation.

Despite the important contributions of Hairston & Oliver's (2006) research, one important question remained unanswered. What are the experiences of formerly incarcerated African American women and their partners in regards to intimate partner violence? Hairston & Oliver's (2006) study did not include formerly incarcerated women; therefore, an understanding of women's experiences was unavailable. The findings presented in this study extend the literature on prisoner reentry and intimate partner violence and the findings of Hairston & Oliver (2006) regarding formerly incarcerated African American men's experiences of intimate partner violence. Hairston and Oliver (2006), revealed the sources of conflict in intimate relationships; however, this study revealed the nature of such violence between formerly incarcerated African American men and women. By comparing African American men's and women's experiences of IPV and the role race, gender, and class play in shaping those experiences, these findings broadened our understanding of how they experience such violence. In doing so, their experiences move beyond the narrow boundaries of the current discourse on prisoner reentry and allow consideration of issues that are often avoided or not discussed.

FUTURE RESEARCH

The narratives and accounts presented herein arguably demonstrate the need to further explore and determine what works best for African American men and women engaged in reentry in terms of violence prevention. In short, further empirical research is needed to understand how race, gender, and class shape African American men's and women's experiences of intimate partner violence, especially for African American women. Research in this area should examine more deeply the experiences and perspectives of formerly incarcerated women who have experienced intimate partner violence after they have returned to the community from prison. It is important that the most typical sources of conflict for women involved in intimate relationships are identified. Future research is needed to create a comprehensive picture of the magnitude and range of intimate partner violence that actually occurs in the lives of once-incarcerated men and women reentering society. Furthermore, more research is needed to find solutions to reduce the risks of intimate partner violence between formerly incarcerated African American men and women, and their partners. Incorporating the voices of formerly incarcerated men and women is crucial towards that effort, as is differentiating which particular restorative justice approach works best during reentry to improve recidivism outcomes and reduce the danger of victimization for African American men and women.

CONCLUSIONS

Reentry is the inevitable consequence of imprisonment. The majority of African American men and women who are sent to prison will one day return to our local communities. Many who leave prison today do not manage to reintegrate successfully back into society. They face multiple competing demands, difficult challenges, and for some the added harm of social inequality. During reentry, negotiating relationships can be extremely difficult and, in many instances, the effort to reconnect can result in intimate partner violence. For this particular population, involvement in intimate partner violence is problematic for several reasons. The majority of men and women released from prison remain under correctional supervision after they return to society and perpetrating intimate partner violence is a violation of conditions of probation and parole supervision. Consequently, the inability of African American men and women to adjust and reintegrate successfully can increase their likelihood of recidivating, returning to prison, or becoming a victim.

The theoretical orientations of restorative justice, critical race theory, and critical race feminism informed this research. Collectively, these three theories assisted with understanding the ways in which race, gender, and class intersect to structure the experiences of IPV of African American men and women during reentry and aided in providing plausible solutions to address this issue. Intimate partner violence prevention programs that are based on restorative justice principles that consider the insights of critical race theory and critical race feminism have the potential to address the multiple issues of formerly incarcerated African American men and women. The failure to address intimate partner violence during reentry can place victims of IPV in continual danger and increase the risk of formerly incarcerated individuals returning to prison.

The goal of this book has been to explore formerly incarcerated African American men and women's experiences of intimate partner violence during reentry. Given the findings of this study, an intimate partner violence prevention program that is based on the principles of restorative justice offers a plausible solution. Restorative justice promotes the overall health and well being of those involved, conditions which have physical, emotional, and mental dimensions. Restorative justice requires attention to the network of relationships and circumstances in which individuals are embedded. With this orientation, the structures, conditions, and connections that influence the well-being of individuals cannot be ignored (Harris, 2004). IPV prevention programs that take into consideration the role of race, gender, and class will have great potential for everyone involved. As the prison population continues to grow, which disproportionately consists of African Americans, it becomes imperative to understand how convicted felons released from custody reintegrate back into society. This problem requires comprehensive policy attention. As this research has shown, addressing the challenges that African American men and women encounter during reentry is imperative to improving their hopes for successful reintegration and ultimately reducing their risk of recidivism and victimization.

Appendix A

Staff Interview Guide

1. So tell me what you do around here.
    o   What is your position?
    o   How long have you worked at the Fortune Society?
2. What is the scope of your responsibilities?
3. What programs and services do the Fortune Society offer?
4. What do you think are the major issues and problems associated with reentry?
   Now I want to turn specifically to intimate partner violence.
5. What do you think are the major issues and problems associated with intimate partner violence?
6. What if any, are some of the barriers in addressing the needs?
7. What are the specific strategies and programs to address IPV and their assessments?
8. From your perspective, do men and women experience intimate partner violence differently during the reentry process?
   If so, in what ways?
   What are those differences?
9. From your perspective, do African American men and women experience intimate partner violence differently than other groups during the reentry process?
   If so, in what ways?
10. Do you have a sense if violence is occurring in the lives of formerly incarcerated men and women you work with?
   If so, how do they deal with the violence?
11. What racial/ethnic group do you identify with?

12. Is there anything that I should have asked that I didn't ask regarding African American men's and women's experiences of intimate partner violence?
13. Who else do you think I should talk to?
14. If there are any questions that I may think of later would it be okay to send a email or give you a call?

Appendix B

Interview Guide

Background
1. Tell me about yourself.
2. Tell me about your childhood.
     a. Where did you grow up?
     b. Who did you live with?
     c. What do you remember about your childhood?
     d. How would you describe your childhood?
     e. Talk about your relationship with your mother.
     f. Talk about your relationship with your father.
     g. Did you witness any violence as a child?
     h. Can you remember your first experience dealing with violence?
          i. Level of your participation?
          ii. Perpetrator of violence? Why did you resort to violence?

Now I would like to ask some questions about your experiences with crime and the criminal justice system.

Involvement with crime and CJS
3. Can you tell me about the first crime you ever committed?
     a. How old were you?
4. How many times have you been arrested?
     a. Circumstances of those arrests?
5. How many times have you been convicted of a crime?
6. What offense(s) were you charged with that led to your last incarceration?
7. Can you tell me about the crime you recently served time for?

8. How long were you sentenced to prison?
   Were you employed when you were arrested?
   Did you have any substance abuse problems?
   Mental health issues?

Prison experience/ environment/culture
9. Where did you do your time?
10. What was a typical day like in prison?
11. Did you experience or witness any violence in prison?
12. Was race an issue in prison?
    a. How did you see that getting played out?
13. Were there any gangs in prison?
    a. Where you involved? If so why?
14. Did you receive visits from your family and friends while you were incarcerated?
    a. If so, who visited you while you were in prison?
    b. How often did s/he/they visit?
15. Do you think your relationships with other people have changed because you have served time in prison?
    a. If yes, in what ways?
16. While incarcerated were you involved in a meaningful relationship with someone in society?
    a. If yes, how was the relationship affected by your incarceration?
17. Has doing time in prison changed your life?
    a. If so, how?

Preparation for release
18. Did you participate in any pre release programs?
19. What was the most important activity?
20. When/how did you find out you were being released?
    a. Did you complete your sentence?
    b. If paroled, how many times did you go up before the parole board?
        i. At the last parole hearing, did you believe you were going to be approved?
        ii. If so, why?

Now I would like to talk in general about what you remember when you left prison.

Release

21. Can you describe the first 24 hours when you were released from prison?
    *PROMPTS
    a. How did you get to your destination?
    b. Where did you stay initially?
    c. What were some of your thoughts and feelings during that time?
    d. Did you feel prepared?
    e. What did you do in the first few hours you were released?
22. Who did you spend the most time with when you first got out of prison?
23. Did you return to your same neighborhood?
24. Did you talk to anyone about your prison experiences?
25. Can you explain some of the obstacles you faced when you were released from prison?
    *PROMPTS
    a. Can you give specific examples?
    b. How did you deal with these challenges?
26. How did you get set-up with…
    a. housing? employment? healthcare?
27. What did you find most challenging when you returned home?
28. Has race played a part in your reentry experience?
    a. If so, how did you know race was the reason?
29. Have you been placed in a position where you thought you would compromise your parole, probation, or freedom?
    a. If so, how did you handle it?
30. *Do you think race played a role in shaping your reentry experience?*
31. *From your perspective, do African American men and women experience the reentry process differently than other groups?*

So now I want to focus specifically on your significant relationship that you have been involved in since release.

Relationship

32. Are you currently involved in an intimate relationship? If not, tell me about your last intimate relationship.
    a.   How long have you been/were in this relationship?
    b.   Were you involved in this relationship while incarcerated?
    c.   Tell me about the person you were in a relationship with?
    d.   Tell me about the relationship.
    e.   Did your incarceration impact your relationship?

Violence

33. Has the process of reentry created a source of conflict or tension between you and your partner?
    a.   Do you believe your partner contributes to the conflict?
    b.   *Do you think being unemployed/underemployed plays a part in this?*
    c.   *I'm trying to understand this, has race played a part in your reentry experience?*
         i.   *If so, how did you know race was the reason?*
34. Have you and your partner cursed each other out, called each other names, or been involved in disrespectful behavior?
    a.   If so, how did you deal with this?
35. Given all the stress coming out of prison, have you been in violent situations with your partner?
    a.   If so who initiated?
    b.   How many times? Once, twice etc.
    c.   How do you deal with this?
36. What is intimate partner violence?
    a.   Do you believe race plays a role in intimate partner violence?
37. Have you ever been a victim of violence as an adult?
38. How do you define violence?
39. What constitutes threatening behavior?
40. What would you define as threatening behavior?
    a.   Hitting
    b.   Slapping

      c.   Pushing

      d.   Kicking

41. Have you ever hit, slapped, pushed, kicked, or hurt your partner?
42. How long does it take before violence becomes an unacceptable behavior?
    a. What is acceptable and what is not?
43. Do you know of any other formerly incarcerated individuals who have engaged in violence with their partners?
    a. Is there someone they can talk to about violence?
44. What does it mean to be black?
45. What does it mean to be a black man/woman?
46. Is there anything else that you would like to tell me that would help me understand your experiences?

References

Allen, A. L. (1997). On being a role model. In A. Wing (Ed.), *Critical race feminism: A reader* (pp.81-87). New York: New York University Press.

Alexander, M. (2010). *The new Jim crow: Mass incarceration in the age of colorblindness.* New York: The New Press.

Andersen, M.L. & Collins, P.H. (2006). *Race, Class, and Gender: An Anthology* (6th ed.). Belmont, CA: Cengage Learning.

Anderson, T.L. (2003). Issues in the availability of health care for women prisoners. In S.F. Sharp (Ed.), *The incarcerated woman: Rehabilitative programming in women's prisons* (pp. 49-60). Upper Saddle River, NJ: Prentice Hall.

Baer, D., Bhati, A., Brooks, L., Castro, J., La Vigne, N., Mallik-Kane, K. et al. (2006). *Understanding the challenges of prisoner reentry: Research findings from the Urban Institute's prisoner reentry portfolio.* Washington, D.C.: The Urban Institute.

Barak, G., Flavin, J., & Leighton, P. S. (2001). *Class, race, gender, and crime: Social realities of justice in America.* Los Angeles: Roxbury.

Baugh, S., Bull, S., & Cohen, C. (1998). Mental health issues, treatment, and the female offender. In R.T. Zaplin (Ed.), *Female offenders: Critical perspectives and effective interventions* (pp. 205-226). Gaithersburg, MD: Aspen.

Bazemore, G. (1999). Crime victims, restorative justice and juvenile court: Exploring victim needs and involvement in the response to youth crime. *International Review of Victimology, 6,* 295-320.

Bazemore, G. (2005). Whom and how do we reintegrate? Finding community in restorative justice. *Criminology & Public Policy, 4*(1), 131-148.

Bazemore, G. & Umbreit, M.S. (2001). *A comparison of four restorative conferencing models.* Washington, D.C.: U. S. Department of Justice, Office of Justice Programs, Office of Juvenile Justice and Delinquency Prevention.

Bazemore, G., & Walgrave, L. (1999). *Restorative juvenile justice: Repairing the Harm of Youth Crime.* Monsey, NY: Criminal Justice Press.

Bederman, G. (1995). *Manliness and civilization: A cultural history of gender and race in the United States, 1880-1917.* Chicago: The University of Chicago Press.

Belknap, J. (2001). *The invisible woman: Gender, crime, and justice* (2nd ed.). Belmont, CA: Wadsworth.

Benedict, W. R., Huff-Corzine, L. & Corzine, J. (1998). Clean up and go straight: Effects of drug treatment on recidivism among felony probationers. *American Journal of Criminal Justice 22*, 169–87.

Benson, M. L., Fox, G. L., Demaris, A., & Van Wyk, J. (2000). Violence in families: The intersection of race, poverty, and community context. In G. L. Fox & M. L. Benson (Eds.), *Families, crime, and criminal justice* (pp. 91-109). New York: JAI.

Benson, M.L., & Fox, G. L. (2004). *When violence hits home: How economics and neighborhood play a role.* Research in Brief. Washington, D.C.: National Institute of Justice, U.S. Department of Justice.

Bent-Goodley, T.B. (2005). Culture and practice: An African-centered approach to domestic violence. *Families in Society: The Journal of Contemporary Social Services, 86,* 197-206.

Bent-Goodley, T.B. (2003). Policy implications of the criminal justice system for African American families and communities. In T.B. Bent-Goodley (Ed.), *African American social workers and social policy* (pp. 137-161). New York: Routledge.

Bent-Goodley, T.B. (2001). Eradicating domestic violence in the African American community: A literature review and action agenda. *Trauma, Violence, & Abuse, 2* (4), 316-330.

Bernstein, J., & Houston, E. (2000) *Crime and Work: What we can learn from the low-wage labor market.* Washington D.C.: Economic Policy Institute.

Bloom, B. (1993). Incarcerated mothers and their children: Maintaining family ties. In *Female offenders: Meeting the needs of a neglected population* (pp. 60-68). Laurel, MD: American Correctional Association.

Bobbitt, M., Campbell, R., & Tate, G.L. (2006). *Safe Return: Working toward preventing domestic violence when men return from prison.* New York: Vera Institute of Justice.

Braithwaite, J. (2002). *Restorative justice and responsive regulation.* New York: Oxford University Press.

Braithwaite, J. (1989). *Crime, Shame and Reintegration.* Cambridge University Press.

Braithwaite, J. (1994). *Crime, Shame, and Reintegration.* New York: Cambridge University Press.

Braithwaite, J. (1999). Restorative Justice: Assessing optimistic and pessimistic accounts. In M. Tonry (Ed.), *Crime and justice: A review of research* (pp. 1-127). Chicago, IL: The University of Chicago Press.

Brewster, D.R. (2003). Does rehabilitative justice decrease recidivism for women prisoners in Oklahoma? In S.F. Sharp (Ed.), *The incarcerated woman: Rehabilitative programming in women's prisons* (pp. 29-45). Upper Saddle River, NJ: Prentice Hall.

Britton, D. M. (2004). Feminism in criminology: Engendering the outlaw. In P. J. Schram & B. Koons-Witt (Eds.), *Gendered (in)justice: Theory and practice in feminist criminology* (pp. 49-67). Long Grove, IL: Waveland Press.

Buckler, K. G., & Travis, L. F. (2003). Reanalyzing the prevalence and social context of collateral consequence statutes. *Journal of Criminal Justice, 31*(5), 435-453.

Bureau of Labor Statistics. *The employment situation-April 2012.* United States Department of Labor.

Bureau of Labor Statistics. *The employment situation-June 2009.* United States Department of Labor.

Campbell, J.C., Webster, D., Koziol-McLain, J., Block, C.R., Campbell, D.,Curry, M.A. et al. (2003). Risk factors for femicide in abusive relationships: Results from a multi-site case control study. *American Journal of Public Health, 93,* 1089-1097.

Campbell, D., Sharps, P., Gary, F., Campbell, J., & Lopez, L. (2002). Intimate partner violence in African American women. *Online Journal of Issues in Nursing.7 (1),* Manuscript 4.

Campbell, J. C., & Soeken, K. L. (1999).Women's responses to battering over time: An analysis of change. *Journal of Interpersonal Violence, 14, 21-40.*

Carson, E.A., & Golinelli D. (2013). *Prisoners in 2012.* United States Department of Justice. Office of Justice Programs. Bureau of Justice Statistics. Washington, D.C.: Government Printing Office.

Carson, E.A., & Sabol, W. (2012). *Prisoners in 2011.* United States Department of Justice. Office of Justice Programs. Bureau of Justice Statistics. Washington, D.C.: Government Printing Office.

Cazenave, N., & Straus, M. A. (1979). Race, class, network embeddedness and family violence: A search for potent support systems. *Journal of Comparative Family Studies, 10,* 281-300.

Cazenave, N., & Straus, M. A. (1990). Race, class, network embeddedness and family violence: A search for potent support systems. In M. A. Strauss & R. J. Gelles (Eds.), *Physical violence in American families* (pp. 320-339). Brunswick, NJ: Transaction.

Centers for Disease Control and Prevention. (2012). Understanding intimate partner violence: Factsheet. Atlanta, Georgia. Centers for Disease Control and Prevention. (2003). *Costs of intimate partner violence against women in the United States.* Atlanta, Georgia.

Centers for Disease Control and Prevention. (2000). Building data systems for   monitoring and responding to violence against women: recommendations   from a workshop. *Morbidity and Mortality Weekly Report 49,* 1-16.

Chesney-Lind, M. (1997). *The female offender: Girls, women, and crime.* Thousand Oaks, CA: Sage.

Christie, N. (1977). Conflicts as property. *British Journal of Criminology, 17* (1), 1-15.

Clear, T. (2006). Community justice versus restorative justice: Contrasts in family of values. In D. Sullivan & L. Tifft (Eds.). *Handbook of Restorative Justice: A Global Perspective* (pp. 463-471). London: Taylor and Francis.

Clear, T. R. (2002). The problem with addition by subtraction: The prison-crime relationship in Low-Income Communities. In M. Mauer & M. Chesney-Lind (Eds.), *Invisible Punishment: The collateral consequences of mass imprisonment* (pp. 181-193). New York: New Press.

Clear, T. R. (1996). *The Unintended Consequences of Incarceration.* Washington, D.C.: National Institute of Justice.

Clear, T.R. & Cadora, E. (2003). *Community Justice*. Belmont, CA: Wadsworth Press.

Clear, T.R., Cole, G.F., Reisig, M.D., & Petrosino, C. (2012). *American Corrections in Brief*. Belmont, CA: Wadsworth Press.

Clear, T.R., Rose, D.R. & Ryder, J.A. (2001). Incarceration and the community: The problem of removing and returning offenders. *Crime and Delinquency 47, (3),* 335-351.

Cohen, M.A. (1988). Pain, suffering, and jury awards: A study of the cost of crime to victims. *Law and Society Review, 22* (3), 537-555.

Collins, P. H. (2006). *From black power to hip hop: Racism, nationalism, and feminism.* Philadelphia: Temple University Press.

Collins, P. H. (2000) *Black feminist thought.* New York: Routledge.

Collins, P. H. (2005). *Black sexual politics: African American gender and new racism.* New York: Routledge.

Collins, P. H. (1998). The tie that binds: Race, gender and U.S. violence. *Ethnic and Racial Studies, 21,* 917-938.

Crenshaw, K. W. (2000). *The intersectionality of race and gender discrimination.* Paper presented at the Expert Group Meeting on Gender & Race Discrimination, Zagreb, Croatia, November 21-24, 2000.

Crenshaw, K. W. (1993). Demarginalizing the intersection of race and sex: A Black feminist critique of antidiscrimination doctrine, feminist theory and antiracist politics. In K. Weisburg (Ed.), *Feminist Legal Theory* (pp. 383-395). Philadelphia: Temple University Press.

Crenshaw, K. W. (1991). Mapping the margins: Intersectionality, identity politics, and violence against women of color. *Stanford Law Review,* 43, (6), 1241-1279.

Crenshaw, K.W. (1989). Demarginalizing the intersectional of race and sex: A Black feminist critique of antidiscrimination doctrine, feminist theory and antiracist politics. *The University of Chicago Legal Forum,* 139-167.

Daly, K. (2003). Mind the gap: Restorative justice in the theory and practice. In   V. Hirsh, A., Roberts, J., Bottoms, A., Roach, K., Schiff (Eds.). *Restorative justice and criminal justice* (pp. 219-237). Portland, OR: Hart Publishing, Oxford and Portland.

Daly, K., & Chesney-Lind, M. (1988). Feminism and criminology. *Justice Quarterly,* 5, 497-538.

Daly, K., & Immarigeon, R. (1998). The past, present, and future of restorative justice: Some critical reflections. *Contemporary Justice Review, 1* (1), 21-45.

Daly, K., & Stubbs, J. (2006). Feminist engagement with restorative justice. *Theoretical Criminology, 10* (1), 9-28.

Danner, T.A., Blount, W.R., Silverman, I.J., & Vega, M. (1995). The female chronic offender: Exploring life contingency and offense history dimensions for incarcerated female offenders. *Women and Criminal Justice, 6* (2), 45-66.

Davis, A. (1981). *Women, Race and Class.* New York: Random House.

Delgado, R., & Stefancic, J. (2001). *Critical race theory: An introduction.* New York University Press.

DeLisi, M. & Conis, P. J. (2013). *American Corrections*: *Theory, Research, Policy, and Practice, Second Edition.* Sudbury, MA: Jones & Bartlett.

DeLisi, M. & Conis, P. J. (2010). *American Corrections*: *Theory, Research, Policy, and Practice.* Sudbury,   MA: Jones & Bartlett.

Dignan, J. (2003). Towards a systematic model of restorative justice: Reflections on the concept, its context and the need for clear constraints.   In A. von Hirsch, J. Roberts, A.E. Bottoms, K. Roach and M. Schiff (Eds.). *Restorative justice and criminal justice: Competing of reconcilable paradigms?* Oxford: Hart Publishing.

Dutton, M.A., Goodman, L., & Schmitt, R. J. (2006). *Development and validation of a coercive Control measure for intimate partner violence.* Final Report to National Institute of Justice. Washington, D.C.: U.S. Department of Justice, Office of Justice Programs.

Edin, K., & Kefalas, M. (2005). *Promises I can keep: Why poor women put motherhood before marriage.* Berkeley: University of California Press.

Evez, E. (1992). Dangerous men, evil women: Gender and parole decision making. *Justice Quarterly, 9,* 105-126.

Fagan, J. (1996). *The criminalization of domestic violence: Promises and limits.* National Institute of Justice Report. Washington, DC: U.S. Department of Justice, Office of Justice Programs.

Failinger, M.A. (2006). Lessons unlearned: Women offenders, the ethics of care, and the promise of restorative justice. *Fordham Urban Law Journal, 33,* 487-527.

Fattah (1998). A critical assessment of two justice paradigms: Contrasting   restorative and retributive justice models. In E.,

Fattah, T. Peters (Eds.). *Support for crime victims in a comparative perspective.* Leuven: Leuven University Press, 99-110.

Fishman, L. T. (1990). *Women at the wall: A study of prisoners' wives doing time on the outside.* Albany, NY: State University of New York Press.

Fogel, R. W., & Engerman S. L. (1974). *Time on the cross: The economics of American Negro slavery.* Boston: Little, Brown.

Frazier, E.F. (1939). *The Negro family in the United States.* Chicago: The University of Chicago Press.

Frost, N., Greene, J., & Pranis, K. (2006). *Hard hit: The growth in the imprisonment of women, 1977-2004.* New York: Institute on Women and Criminal Justice, Women's Prison Association.

Gaes, G., Flanagan, T.J., Motluk, L.L., & Stewart, L. (1999). Adult correctional treatment. In M. Tonry., & J. Petersilla (Eds.), *Prisons* (pp. 361-426). Chicago: The University of Chicago Press.

Garfield, G. (2010). *Through our eyes: African American men and women's experiences of race, gender, and violence.* New Brunswick, New Jersey: Rutgers University Press.

Garfield, G. (2005) *Knowing what we know: African American women's experiences of violence and violation.* New Jersey: Rutgers University Press.

Gelles, R.J., & Strauss M.A. (1990). The medical and psychological costs of family violence. In M.A, Strauss & R.J. Gelles (Eds.), *Physical violence in American families: Risk factors in adaptations to violence in 8,145 families* (pp. 425-30). New Brunswick, NJ: Transaction Publishers.

Gilfus, M.E. (1992). From victims to survivors to offenders: Women's routes of entry and immersion into street crime. *Women and Criminal Justice,* 4, 63-90.

Glaser, B. G., & Strauss, A. L. (1967). *The discovery of grounded theory.* Chicago: Aldine Publishing Company.

Greene, J. P., Winters, M.A., & Manhattan Institute for Policy Research. (2005). *Public high school graduation and college-readiness rates, 1991-2002.* New York: Manhattan Institute for Policy Research, Center for Civic Innovation.

Greene, S., Haney, C., & Hurtado, A. (2000). Cycles of pain: Risk
  factors in the lives of incarcerated mothers and their children. *The
  Prison Journal, 80 (1),* 3-23.

Guerino, P., Harrison, P.M., & Sabol, W. J. (2011). *Prisoners in 2010.*
  U.S. Department of Justice. Washington, D.C.: Office of Justice
  Programs. Gutman, H.G. (1976). *The black family in slavery and
  freedom, 1750-1925.* New York: Pantheon.

Hairston, C. & Oliver, W. (2006). *Domestic violence and prisoner
  reentry: Experiences of African American men and women.* New
  York: Vera Institute of Justice.

Hallet, M. (2011). Reentry to what? Theorizing prisoner reentry
  in the jobless future. *Critical Criminology 20,* 213-228.

Hammett, T.M., Roberts, S. & Kennedy, S. (2001). Health related
  issues in prisoner reentry to the community. *Crime and
  Delinquency 47,* (3), 390-409.

Hampton, R., Carillo, R., & Kim, J. (1998). Violence in communities
  of color. In R. Carillo & J. Tello (Eds.), *Family violence and men
  of color: Healing the wounded male spirit* (pp. 1-30). New York:
  Springer Publishing Company.

 Hampton, R. L., & Gelles, R. J. (1994). Violence toward Black women
  in a nationally representative sample of Black families. *Journal of
  Comparative Family Studies, 25,* 105-120.

Hanser, R. (2010). *Community Corrections.* Belmont, CA: Sage
  Publications.

Harlow, C. (2003). *Education and correctional populations.*
  Washington D.C.: Bureau of Justice Statistics.

Harm, N.J., & Phillips, S.D. (2001). You can't go home again: Women
  and criminal recidivism. *Journal of Offender Rehabilitation, 32*(3),
  3-21.

Harris, A. P. (1990). Race and essentialism in feminist legal theory.
  Stanford Law Review 42.3, 581-616.

Harrison, P.M., & Beck, A.J. (2006). *Prison and jail inmates at
  midyear, 2005.* Washington, D.C.: U.S. Department of Justice,
  Bureau of Justice Statistics.

Hattery, A.J. (2007). *African American families.* Sage Publications.

Hemmens, C. & Marquart, J.W. (2000). Friend or foe? Race, age, and
  inmate perceptions of inmate staff relations. *Journal of Criminal
  Justice, 28,*   297-312.

Hepburn, J., & Albonetti, C. (1980). Role conflict in correctional institutions: An empirical examination of the treatment-custody dilemma among correctional staff. *Criminology, 17*, 445-459.

Holtfreder, K., & Morash, M. (2003). The needs of women offenders: Implications for correctional programming. *Women and Criminal Justice, 14(23)*, 137-160.

Holzer, H., Raphael, S., & Stoll M. (2004). Will employers hire former offenders? Employers preferences, background checks, and their determinants. In B. Western, M. Patillo., & D. Welman (Eds.), *Imprisoning America: The social effects of mass incarceration.* New York: The Russell Sage Foundation.

Hooks, b. (1989). *Talking back: Thinking feminist, thinking Black.* Boston: South End.

Hooks, b. (2004). *We real cool: Black men and masculinity.* New York: Routledge.

Hudson, B. (2003). Victims and Offenders. In V. Hirsh, A. Roberts, J. Bottoms, A. Roach, K. Schiff (Eds.), *Restorative Justice and Criminal Justice* (pp. 177-195). Portland, OR: Hart Publishing, Oxford and Portland.

James, D. J., & Glaze, L.E. (2006). Mental health problems of prison and jail inmates. Bureau of Justice Statistics: Special Report.

Joseph, J. (1997). Women battering: A comparative analysis of Black and White women. In G.K. Kantor & J.L. Jasinkski (Eds.), *Out of darkness: Contemporary perspectives on family violence* (pg 161-169). Thousand Oaks, CA: Sage.

Karp, D.R., & Clear, T. R. (2002). *What is Community Justice?* Thousand Oaks, CA: Pine Forge Press.

Krug, E. G., Dahlberg, L. L., Mercy, J. A., Zwi, A. B., & Lozano, R. (2002). *World report on violence and health.* Geneva, Switzerland: World Health Organization.

Langan, P., & Levin, D. (2002). *Recidivism of prisoners released in 1994.* Bureau of Justice Statistics Special Report. Washington, D.C.: U.S. Department of Justice.

Langford, D. R. (1996). Policy issues for improving institutional response to domestic violence. *Journal of Nursing Administration, 26*, 39-45.

Latimer, J., Dowden, C., & Muise, D. (2001). *The effectiveness of restorative justice practices: A meta-analysis.* Ottawa: Department of Justice.

Lemelle, A. J. (1995). *Black male deviance.* Westport, CT: Praeger Publishers.

Lurigio, A.J. (2000). Drug treatment availability and effectiveness. *Criminal Justice and Behavior, 27*(4), 495-528.

Lynch, J.P., Sabol, W. J., Planty, M., & Shelley, M. (2001). *Crime, coercion, and community: The effects of arrest and incarceration policies on   informal social control in neighborhoods.* Report to the National Institute of Justice. Washington, D.C.

Marbley, A. F. & Ferguson, R. (2005). Responding to prisoner reentry, recidivism, and incarceration of inmates of color: A call to communities. *Journal of Black Studies, 35 (*5), 633-649.

Marshall, T., & Merry, S. (1990). *Crime and accountability: Victim offender in practice.* London: HMSO.

Marshall, C. & Rossman, G.V. (1989). *Designing Qualitative Research.* California: Sage Publications.

Martin, L. (203). Reentry within the carceral: Foucault, race, and prisoner reentry. *Critical Criminology, 2,* 493-508.

Matusda, M. J. (1992). When the first quail calls: Multiple consciousness as our jurisprudential method, 13 *Women's Rights Law Reporter* 297, 298.

Mauer, M. (2011). Addressing racial disparities in incarceration. *Prison Journal, 91 (3),* 87S-101S.

Mauer, M. (1999). *The race to incarcerate.* New York: New York Press.

Mauer, M., & Chesney-Lind, M. (Eds.). (2002). *Invisible punishment: The collateral consequences of mass imprisonment.* New York: New Press.

Maxwell, J.A. (1996). *Qualitative research design: An interactive approach.* Thousand Oaks, CA: Sage.

Maxwell, G., & Morris, A. (1993). *Family, Victims and Culture: Youth Justice in New Zealand.* Wellington, New Zealand: Social Policy Agency and Institute of Criminology, Victoria University of Wellington.

McCold, P. (2003). *Restorative justice: An annotated bibliography.* Monsey, NY: Criminal Justice Press.

McCold, P. (1996). Restorative justice and the role of community. In, B. Galaway and J. Hudson (Eds.), *Restorative justice: International perspectives* (p. 85-101). Monsey, New York: Criminal Justice Press.

McGarrell, E.F. (2001*). Restorative justice conferences as an early response to young offenders. Juvenile Justice Bulletin* (August). Washington, D.C.: U.S. Department of Justice, Office of Justice Programs, Office of Juvenile Justice and Delinquency Prevention.

Messerschmidt, J. W. (1997). *Crime as structured action: Gender, race, class, and crime in the making.* Thousand Oaks: Sage Publications.

Metraux, S., & Culhane, D.P. (2004). Homeless shelter use and reincarceration following prisoner release: Assessing the risk. *Criminology and Public Policy, 3,* 2001-22.

Meyers, M. (2004). African American women and violence: Gender, race, and class in the news. *Critical Studies in Media Communication, 21,* 95-118.

Miers, D. (2001). An explanatory evaluation of restorative justice schemes, Crime Reduction Policing and Reducing Crime Unit, Research Series Paper 9, London: Home Office.

Miller, S. (2011). *After the crime. The power of restorative justice dialogues between victims and violent offenders.* New York, NY: NYU Press.

Mumola, C. (2000). *Incarcerated parents and their children.* Washington, D.C.: U.S. Department of Justice, Bureau of Justice Statistics.

Mutua, A. D. (Ed.). (2006). *Progressive black masculinities.* New York: Routledge.

Nash, S. T. (2005). Through black eyes: African American women's constructions of their experiences with intimate male partner violence. *Violence Against Women, 11(*11), 1420-1440.

National Governors Association Center for Best Practices (2004). *The challenges and impacts of prisoner reentry.* Washington, D.C.: National Governors Association.

Nicholl, C. G. (1999). *Community policing, community justice, and restorative justice: Exploring the links for the delivery of a balanced approach to public safety.* Washington, D.C.: U.S.

Department of Justice: Office of Community Oriented Policing Services.

O'brien, P. (2001). Just like baking a cake: Women describe the necessary ingredients for successful reentry after incarceration. *Families in Society: The Journal of Contemporary Human Services, 82* (3), 287- 295.

Pager, D. (2003). The mark of a criminal record. *American Journal of Sociology, 108,* 937-975.

Pager, D. (2007). *Marked: Race, crime, and finding work in an era of mass incarceration.* Chicago: The University of Chicago Press.

Peachey, D. E. (1989). What people want from mediation. In K. Kressel, D. G. Pruitt & Associates (Eds.), *Mediation research: The process and effectiveness of third-party intervention* (pp. 300–321). San Francisco: Jossey-Bass.

Pelissier, B., & Jones, N. (2005). A review of gender differences among substance abuse abusers. *Crime & Delinquency, 51*(3), 343-372.

Petersilia, J. (2004). What works in prisoner reentry? Reviewing and questioning the evidence. *Federal Probation, 62,* 2, 4-8.

Petersilia, J. (2003). *When prisoners return to communities: Political, economic and social consequences.* New York: Oxford University Press.

Petersilia, J. & Travis, J. (Eds.) (2001). Special issue: From prison to society: Managing the challenges of prisoner reentry. *Crime and Delinquency, 47 (3),* 291-485.

Pettit, B. & Western, B. (2004). Mass imprisonment and the life course: Race and class inequality in U.S. incarceration. *American Sociological Review, 69* (2), 151-169.

Peugh, J., & Belenko, S. (1999). Substance involved women inmates: Challenges to providing effective treatment. *The Prison Journal, 79,* 23-45.

Potter, H. (2008). *Battle cries: Black women and intimate partner abuse.* New York, NY: NYU Press.

Pranis, K. (1993). Restorative justice: Implications for women offenders. *IARCA Journal on Community Corrections, 5* (6), 10-12.

Radosh, P.F. (2002). Reflections on women's crime and mothers in prison: A peacemaking approach. *Crime & Delinquency, 48*(2), 300-315.

Ragin, C. (1987). *The comparative method: Moving beyond qualitative and quantitative strategies.* Berkeley, CA: University of California Press.

Reeves, H. (1989). The Victim Support Perspective. In M. Wright, B. Galaway (Eds.), *Mediation and Criminal Justice: Victims, Offenders and Community* (pp. 44-56). Sage Publications.

Rennison, C., & Planty M. (2003). Nonlethal intimate partner violence: Examining race, gender, and income patterns. *Violence and Victims, 18,* 433-443.

Rennison, C. M., & Welchans, S. (2002). *Intimate partner violence (NCJ 178247).* Washington, D.C.: U.S. Department of Justice, Bureau of Justice Statistics.

Richie, B. (2001). Challenges incarcerated women face as they return to their Communities: Findings from life history interviews. *Crime & Delinquency 47* (3), 368-389.

Richie, B.E. (1996). *Compelled to crime: The gender entrapment of battered Black Women.* New York: Routledge.

Richie, B. E. (2000). A Black feminist reflection on the anti-violence movement. *Signs 24,* 1133-1138.

Richie, B. E. & Johnson, C. (1996). Gender violence, incarceration and women's health: The prevalence of abuse history among newly incarcerated women in a New York City jail. *Journal of the American Women's Medical Association 52,* (2), 89-93.

Roach, K. (2000). Changing punishment at the turn of the century: Restorative justice on the rise, Du chatiment a la justice reparatrice: une evolution? *Canadian Journal of Criminology, 42* (3), 250-280.

Robbins, C.A., Martin, S. S., & Surratt, H.L. (2009). Substance abuse treatment anticipated maternal roles, and reentry success of drug-involved women prisoners. *Crime & Delinquency, 55* (3), 388-411.

Roberts, T. (1994). When violence hits home. *Health Quest, 5,* 50-53.

Roberts, J., & Roach, K. (2003). Restorative Justice in Canada: From Sentencing Circles to Sentencing Principles. In V. Hirsh, A. Roberts, J. Bottoms, A. Roach, K., Schiff, M. (Eds.), *Restorative Justice and Criminal Justice* (232-256). Portland, OR: Hart Publishing, Oxford and Portland.

Roberts, J. V. (2003). Public opinion and mandatory sentencing: A review of international findings. *Criminal Justice and Behavior, 30*(4), 483–508.

Rome, D. (2004). Black demons: *The media's depiction of the African American male criminal stereotype.* Westport, CT: Praeger.

Rose, D. R., & Clear, T. R. (1998). Incarceration, social capital and crime: Implications for social disorganization theory. *Criminology, 36,* 441-79.

Rose, D. R., Clear, T.R., & Ryder J. A. (2001). Addressing the unintended consequences of incarceration through community-oriented services. *Corrections Management Quarterly, 5*(3), 69-78.

Rose, P. (1974). *They and we: Racial and ethnic relations in the United States.* New York: Random House.

Rubenstein, G., & Mukamal, D. (2002). Welfare and housing: Denial of benefits to drug offenders. In M. Mauer & M. Chesney-Lind (Eds.), *Invisible Punishment: The collateral consequences of mass imprisonment* (pp. 37-49). New York: New Press.

Sabol, W.J., & Couture, H. (2008). *Prison inmates at midyear, 2007.* Washington, D.C.: U.S. Department of Justice, Bureau of Justice Statistics.

Sampson, R. J. (1987). Urban black violence: The effect of male joblessness and family disruption. *American Journal of Sociology, 93,* 348-382.

Sentencing Project: Research and Advocacy Reform. (2006). Felony Disenfranchisement Laws in U.S. Washington, D.C.: Sentencing Project.

Sherman, L., Strang, H., & Woods, D. J. (2000). *Recidivism patterns in the Canberra Reintegrative Shaming Experiments (RISE).* Canberra: Centre for Restorative Justice, Research School of Social Sciences, Australian National University.

Smart, C. (1976). *Women, Crime and Criminology.* London: Routledge.

Snell, T.L. (1994). *Women in prison.* Washington, D.C.: U.S. Department of Justice, Bureau of Justice Statistics.

Snow, D. A., Baker, S. G., & Anderson, L. (1989). Criminality and homeless men: An empirical assessment. *Social Problems, 36,* 532-549.

Sokoloff N. J., & Dupont, I. (2005). Domestic violence at the intersections of race, class, and gender: Challenges and contributions to understanding violence against women in diverse communities. *Violence Against Women, 11*, 38-64.

Sokoloff, N. J. & Pratt, C. (2005). *Domestic Violence at the Margins: Readings in Race, Class, Gender & Culture.* Piscataway, NJ: Rutgers University.

Solomon, A., Roman, C.G., & Waul, M. (2001). *Summary of focusing group with ex-prisoners in the District: Ingredients for successful reintegration.* Washington, D.C.: Urban Institute.

Sorenson, S.B., Upchurch, D.M., & Shen, H. (1996). Violence and injury in marital arguments: Risk patterns and gender differences. *American Journal of Public Health, 86*, 35-40.

Spohn, C., & Holleran, D. (2002). The effect of imprisonment on recidivism rates of felony offenders: A focus on drug offenders. *Criminology 40*, 329-358.

Strang, H., & Braithwaite, J. (Eds.). (2002). *Restorative justice and family violence.* New York: Cambridge University Press.

Strauss, A. (1987). *Qualitative analysis for social scientists.* Cambridge: Cambridge, University Press.

Strauss, A., & Corbin, J. (1990). *Basics of qualitative analysis.* Newbury Park, CA: Sage.

Strauss, M. A., Gelles, R. J., & Steinmetz, S. K. (1980). *Behind Closed Doors: Violence in the American family.* Garden City, New York: Doubleday.

Stubbs, J. (2007). Beyond apology? Domestic violence and critical questionsfor restorative justice. *Criminology and Criminal Justice, 7*(2), 169-187.

Sullivan, E., Mino, M., Nelson, K., & Pope, J. (2002). *Families as resource in recovery from drug abuse: An evaluation of la bodega de la familia.* New York: Vera Institute of Justice.

Taylor-Greene, H., Polzer, K., & Lavin-Loucks, D. (2006). Prisoner reentry and transition in Dallas, Texas. *Williams Review, 1* (1), 37-62.

The Henry J. Kaiser Family Foundation. (2007). *Race, Ethnicity & Health Care Fact Sheet. The Health Status of African American Men in the United States.* Menlo Park, CA: The Henry J. Kaiser Family Foundation.

Tjaden, P., & Thoennes, N. (2006). Tjaden, P. & Thoennes, N. (2006). *Extent, nature, and consequences of rape victimization: Findings from the National Violence Against Women Survey. Special*

Report. Washington, D.C.: National Institute of Justice and the Centers for Disease Control and Prevention.

Tjaden, P., & Thoennes, N. (2000). *Extent, nature, and consequences of intimate partner violence: Findings from the National Violence Against Women Survey.* Washington, D.C.: U.S. Government Printing Office.

Tjaden, P., & Thoennes, N. (1998). *Prevalence, incidence, and consequences of violence against women: Findings from the National Violence Against Women Survey.* Atlanta, GA: Center for Disease Control and Prevention, Center for Injury Prevention and Control.

Travis, J. (2005). *But they all come back: Facing the challenges of prisoner reentry.* Washington D.C.: The Urban Institute Press.

Travis, J. (2000). *But they all come back: Rethinking prisoner reentry.* Washington, D.C.: National Institute of Justice.

Travis, J., Cincotta, E., & Solomon, A.L. (2003). *Families left behind: The hidden costs of incarceration and reentry.* Washington, D.C.: The Urban Institute.

Travis, J., Solomon, A. L., & Waul, M. (2001). *From prison to home: The dimensions and consequences of prisoner reentry.* Washington, D.C.: Urban Institute.

Umbreit, M. S. (1985). *Crime and reconciliation: Creative options for victims and offenders.* Nashville, TN: Abingdon Press.

Umbriet, M. (1994). *Victims meets offender. The impact of restorative and mediation.* Monsey: Criminal Justice Press.

Umbriet, M., Bradshaw, W., & Coates, R. (1999). Victims of severe violence meet the offender: Restorative justice through dialogue. *International Review of Victimology, 6,* 321-345.

Umbreit, M.S., & Zehr, H. (1996). Restorative family group conferences: Differing models and guidelines for practice. *Federal Probation, 60* (3), 24–29.

United States Census Bureau. (2011). *Annual social and economic supplement.* Washington, D.C.

United States Department of Labor, Bureau of Labor Statistics. (2006).

United States Department of Justice (2008). *Prison Inmates at Midyear, 2007.* Bureau of Justice Statistics. Washington, D.C.: U.S. Government Printing Office.

United States Department of Justice. Office on Violence Against Women. Washington, D.C. [cited 2012 January 25] Available from URL http://www.ovw.usdoj.gov/areas-focus.html#dv.

United States Department of Justice (2001). *Correctional populations in the United States, 2000.* Office of Justice Programs, Bureau of Justice Statistics. Washington, D.C.: Government Printing Office.

United States Department of Justice, Office of Justice Programs. (2014). Recidivism of prisoners released in 30 states in 2005: Patterns from 2005-2010. Washington, D.C.: Government Printing Office.

Urban Institute, Justice Policy Center. (2006). *Understanding the challenges of prisoner reentry: Research findings from the Urban Institute's prisoner reentry portfolio.* Washington, D.C.: The Urban Institute.

Van Ness, D. W. (1986). *Crime and its victims.* Downers Grove: InterVarsity Press.

Van Ness, D. W. (1993). New wine and old wineskins: Four challenges of restorative Justice. *Criminal Law Forum, 4* (2), 251-276.

Van Ness, D., & Strong, K.H. (1997). *Restoring justice.* Cincinnati, OH: Anderson.

Van Ness, D., & Strong, K.H. (2015). *Restoring Justice: An introduction to restorative justice 5th Edition.* New Providence, NJ: Anderson.

Van Wormer, K. (2009). Restorative justice as social justice for victims of gendered violence: A standpoint feminist perspective. *Social Work, 54* (2), 107-116.

Visher, C.A. & Travis, J. (2003). Transition from prison to community: Understanding individual pathways. *Annual Review of Sociology, 29,* 89-113.

Walgrave, L. (2003). Imposing restoration instead of inflicting pain. In A. von Hirsch, J. Roberts, A.E. Bottoms, K. Roach and M. Schiff (Eds.), *Restorative justice and criminal justice: Competing or reconcilable paradigms?* Oxford: Hart Publishing.

Washington, P. A. (2001). Disclosure patterns of Black female sexual assault survivors. *Violence Against Women, 7,* 1254-1283.

Websdale, N. (1999). *Understanding domestic homicide.* Boston: Northeastern University Press.

Weitekamp, E. G. (1998). Calculating the damage to be restored: Lessons from the national survey of crime severity. In E. Fattah & T. Peters (Eds.), *Support for crime victims in a comparative perspective* (pp. 219- 228). Leuven, Belgium: Leuven University Press.

Weitzman, B. (1996). The treatment of female offenders: Individual psychotherapy in systems-theory perspective. In R.T. Zaplin (Ed.), *Female offenders: Critical perspectives and effective interventions* (pp. 165-178). Gaithersburg, MD: Aspen.

West, C. (2004). Black women and intimate partner violence: New directions for research. *Journal of Interpersonal Violence, 19,* 1487-1493.

West, C. (2005). Violence in ethnically diverse families: The "political gag order" has been lifted. In N. J. Sokoloff & C. Pratt (Eds.), *Domestic violence at the margins: Readings in race, class, gender, and culture.* Piscataway, NJ: Rutgers University Press.

West, T. (1999). *Wounds of the spirit: Black women, violence, and resistance ethics.* New York: New York University Press.

Western, B. (2006). *Punishment and inequality in America.* New York: Russell Sage Foundation.

Williams, O. (1992). Ethnically sensitive practice to enhance treatment participation of African American men who batter. *Families in Society: The Journal of Contemporary Human Services, 21 (1),* 53-64.

Wilkinson, R.A. (1997). A shifting paradigm: Modern restorative justice principles have their roots in ancient cultures. *Corrections Today,* Editorial, December 2007.

Wilson, W.J. (1996). *When work disappears: The world of the new urban poor.* New York: Knopf.

Wing, A. (1997). *Critical race feminism: A reader.* New York: New York University Press.

Wing, A. (2003). *Critical Race Feminism: A Reader, 2nd Edition.* New York: New York University Press.

Women in Prison Project (2002). *Women in prison fact sheet.* Correctional Association of New York.

Women's Prison Association: WPA focus on women & justice. October 2003.

Women's Prison Association: Women, re-entry, and everyday life: Time to work. March 2008.

Wood, J. T (2001). The normalization of violence in heterosexual romantic relationships: Women's narratives of love and violence. *Journal of Social and Personal Relationships, 18,* 239-262.

Wood, J. T. (2004). Monsters and victims: Male felons' accounts of intimate partner violence. *Journal of Social and Personal Relationships, 21,* 555-576.

Zehr, H. (1985). *Retributive justice, restorative justice. New perspectives on crime and justice (Issue #4).* Akron, PA: Mennonite Central Committee Office of Criminal Justice.

Zehr, H. (1995). Justice paradigm shift? Values and visions in the reform process. *Mediation Quarterly, 12* (3), 207-216.

Zehr, H., & Mika, II. (1998). Fundamental concepts of restorative justice. *Contemporary Justice Review, 1* (1), 47–55.

Index

African Americans, 7, 11, 15, 19, 22-23, 28-30, 32-34, 56, 67, 122, 128

Aggravated assault, 69, 75, 97, 108, 110

Anger, 2, 12, 53-54, 60, 62-66, 118, 124

Armed robbery, 72-73, 79-83, 85-86, 89- 93, 113-114

Bazemore, Gordon, 5, 24-26

Blacks. *See* African American

Burglary, 69, 73-75, 77, 82-83, 97-99, 103, 105, 108, 110, 115

Children, 17, 20, 31, 43, 51, 54, 67-68, 81-86, 91, 101, 103, 111-112, 119-121

Clear, Todd, 3, 5, 11, 14, 16, 19-20, 23-24, 34, 56, 79, 87

Clients, 41-42, 45, 47-55, 57, 59-60, 62-65, 67, 71

Collins, P.H., 7, 28, 37-38

Comparative analysis, 10, 38, 44-45

Conflict, 2, 12, 20, 41, 44, 58-64, 87-92, 96, 103, 105, 110-111, 119, 121, 124-126, 134

Conspiracy, 69, 72-73, 75, 77, 79, 81, 83, 85, 87-88, 92, 95, 106, 114

Conviction, 14, 30-31, 43, 50, 69, 71-75, 79-80, 82, 95, 106

Crenshaw, Kimberle, 37

Criminal behavior, 5, 25, 32, 111, 119, 121

Criminal careers, 69

Criminal record, 14, 16

Criminology, 8

Critical race feminism, 4, 8, 127

Critical race theory, 4, 7-8, 127

Cultural competence, 3, 13

Data collection, 22, 44

Depression, 60, 100

Discrimination, 8, 15, 113

Domestic violence, 2, 13, 21-23, 26, 63-64

Employed, 3, 10, 14, 20-21, 29-31, 48, 51, 79, 97, 110, 117

Family group conferencing, 25

Felony convictions, 30, 69, 71-75, 79-83, 87, 90, 92, 97, 102, 105-106, 110, 114

Fighting, 80, 91, 102, 106, 123

Formerly incarcerated, 2-4, 9-14, 16-19, 21, 27-28, 31-32, 34-35,

37-42, 44, 46-51, 54, 57-63, 66, 95, 101, 107, 111-112, 118-129

Fortune Society, 10, 38-40, 43, 45, 47, 50-51, 53, 55, 57, 63, 67-71, 81, 99, 104, 107, 113, 118, 129

Gang, 69, 71-74, 80, 83, 85-93, 95, 113

Garfield, Gail, 23, 33, 53, 123

Gender, 4, 7-8, 10-13, 15, 21, 29-32, 34-35, 37-38, 41, 43-44, 48, 56, 96, 110-111, 113, 117, 119, 122-123, 125-128

Grounded theory, 43

Hairston, Creasie, 1-2, 11-13, 16, 19-21, 23, 30, 91, 125-126

Health care, 14, 21, 29-30, 117

Homeless, 17

Homicide, 69, 71, 80, 85, 96, 104, 113

Housing, 3, 10, 14, 17, 20-21, 23, 29-31, 38, 43, 48-50, 70-71, 79, 81-82, 96-99, 110-111, 117, 119

Incarceration, 1, 3, 4-5, 7, 10-12, 14, 17, 19-20, 23, 27, 31-32, 38, 41, 58, 60, 69, 71, 99, 101, 103, 109, 111, 117, 119, 121-122, 131-132, 134

Intake data, 10, 39, 43, 45, 67, 71

Intersectionality, 7, 37

Interview, 40-44, 60, 67-70, 81, 98

Intimate partner violence, 2-4, 9-13, 21-23, 26-28, 30, 32-35, 39-40, 42-44, 47-48, 51-58, 61-62, 64-66, 88, 96, 103, 107-109, 117-118, 121-129

Intimate relationships, 32, 41, 57-58, 87-88, 90-91, 96, 103, 109-111, 119-121, 123-124, 126

John Jay College, 40

Manslaughter, 70, 74-75, 97-104, 107

Marketable skills, 49, 79, 96

Mass incarceration, 1

Mental health, 14, 18-19, 67, 97, 100, 110-111, 119

Methods, 39, 45

New York City, 39, 68, 113, 149

Offender, 5-6, 24-28, 33-34, 122

Oliver, William, 1-2, 11-13, 16, 19-21, 23, 30, 88-89, 91, 123, 125-126

Oppression, 7, 32, 37

Parole, 2-3, 12, 24, 63, 70-75, 83, 98, 100-101, 121, 127, 132-133

Perpetrators, 32, 65, 91, 107, 110, 112, 120

Petersilia, Joan, 3, 11, 14, 17, 79, 82

Physical violence, 21, 58, 61, 91, 110, 112, 120

Potter, Hillary, 109

Prison, 1-4, 11-15, 17-20, 27, 30-31, 35, 39-42, 48-49, 51, 56-57, 68-69, 71, 73-75, 80, 85-88, 90, 93, 98-100, 102, 104, 106, 111-114, 117-121, 125-128, 132-134

Prison experience, 87, 113

Prisoner reentry, 1-2, 9, 11, 13, 17, 27, 38, 40, 122, 125

Prisoners, 1-3, 11, 17-19, 32-33, 111

Public policy, 117

Qualitative analysis, 41

Race, 3-4, 7-8, 10-13, 19, 21, 28-38, 41, 43-44, 48, 50, 54-56, 79, 96-98, 110, 113, 117-118, 122-123, 125-128, 132-134

Recidivism, 3, 6, 26, 122, 126, 128

Reentry. *See* prisoner reentry

Relationship, 2, 7-8, 11, 20, 26, 39, 41, 43, 52, 58, 61, 64, 68, 83, 85, 87-89, 91-94, 101, 103-108, 111-112, 119-122, 131-134

Restorative justice, 4-9, 24-28, 34, 121, 124, 126-127

Richie, Beth, 1, 8, 11, 18, 21, 30, 103

Robbery, 69, 72-77, 79-80, 87, 90, 93, 95, 97

Sale of a controlled substance, 72-73, 76, 82, 85, 92, 106, 114

Sentencing circles, 25

Social inequalities, 4, 7, 35

Social Services, 97, 107, 115

Sokoloff, Natalie, 23

Solitary confinement, 87, 113

Struggle, 1, 15, 100, 109, 115

Survivor, 27

Trauma, 57

Travis, Jeremy, 3, 11, 16, 20, 28, 30

Treatment, 14-15, 17, 20-21, 23, 100

Unemployment, 1, 15, 31, 34-35, 81, 121

Verbally abusive, 104

Victims, 2, 4-7, 13, 21-22, 24-29, 32-34, 57, 66, 91, 96, 108-112, 120, 127, 134

Violence, 2-4, 8, 11-13, 21-23, 26-27, 30-34, 37, 41, 44, 52-54, 56-66, 72, 88-89, 91, 93-96, 103-104, 105-108, 110, 112, 117-118, 120-127, 129-132, 134-135

Violent, 5, 26, 56, 59, 69, 71, 91, 97, 107, 112, 120, 134

Women, 1-4, 7-18, 20-23, 26-35, 38-40, 42-51, 53-60, 62-64, 66-71, 82, 85, 87, 93-113, 115, 117-127, 129, 133